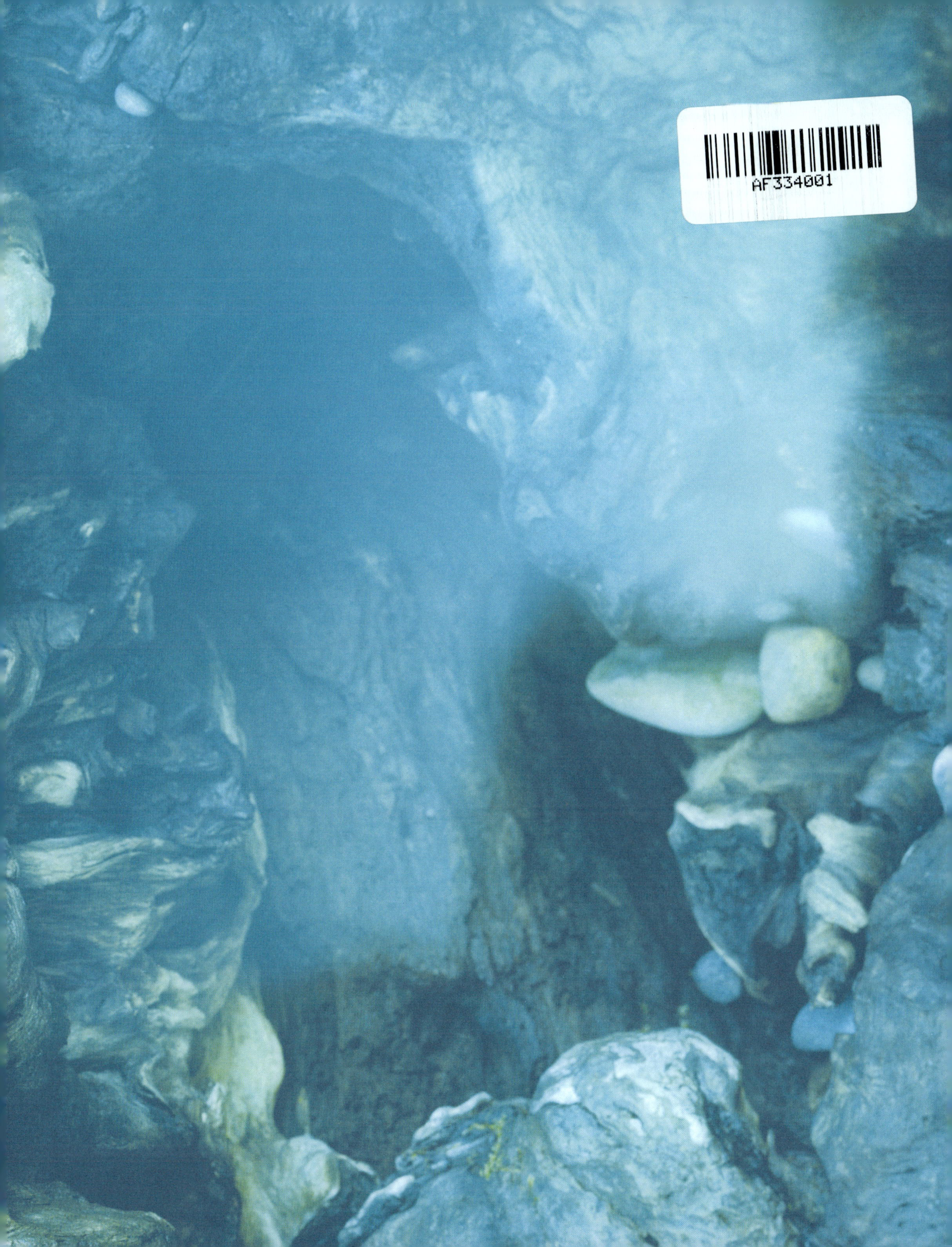
AF334001

DAVID BENJAMIN SHERRY

QUANTUM LIGHT

When David Benjamin Sherry arrived at Yale for graduate school in 2006, he found a mentor in Collier Schorr. Now that both are based in New York, they remain in conversation.

Collier Schorr: Has the way we think about color changed?

David Benjamin Sherry: Absolutely. I think color seems unable to surprise people or to have that visceral impact it may have had in art in the past. The computer has also shifted our associations with color. Digital color can appear wildly extreme, but it always loses me in the end. I'm interested in a kind of surreal extremity, but one that's tied to reality. I like the reality of photography, the connection to the tangible. It's nice to think about color itself in the abstract, but it's almost impossible from brain to eye, and I think that's part of the reason many people are frightened by color.

What about our ideas of hard and soft? When I first saw your work, I thought about Kenneth Anger and the way he made the motorcycle soft, almost melting it with his own desire.

Our ideas of hard and soft are malleable everywhere. Consciously, socially, we are constantly conditioning them through what we see and feel. In photography, "hard" images seem less shocking these days. They usually end up feeling contrived or they elicit a kind of antithetical softness. It seems easier to make something soft rather than hard.

Kenneth Anger influenced a lot of my early work and will always resonate. I thank you, Collier, for really bringing my attention to his work within my first few weeks of graduate school and in my early stages of coming out. Anger eroticized everything he filmed, from the motorcycle to the harsh desert landscape. He incorporated so many elements of hard and soft, literally and metaphorically, like the long romantic shots of Scorpio lying on his bed reading comics, surrounded by pictures of James Dean and motorcycles in *Scorpio Rising*, or slowly getting high and primping his leather jacket and jeweled skull rings with girl groups blasting the airwaves.

Robert Mapplethorpe also dealt with this in an interesting way. By photographing explicit subject matter in his early work and then flowers in his later work, he made hard and soft quite literal. Simply by placing graphic sexuality alongside budding flowers, he raised the bar high — maybe too high. The simple contrast was so new and so charged, and he owned it. He still does. It's hard to imagine anyone working in that extremity nowadays and being successful at it.

I want apocalyptic versions of simple reality, I want beauty joined with disgust, that seems hard yet soft at the same time. Despite all this, it's difficult to define hard and soft precisely — thanks in part to the computer. The Internet has opened the door to overtly hard images that are difficult to one-up or even converse with as an image-maker. It has an immediacy that no single person can keep up with. Soft is easier to speak about since it's where our society is. As a culture maybe we're growing numb. We're angry, but we're pacified by virtual comforts. Sometimes that thought alone pushes me to make things, to move beyond the computer, to go taste the sea and touch the soil.

I asked you about color and about hard and soft because I think of words like "flaming" and "lavender" when I look at your work and those words also have a hard and a soft connotation. Is it wrong to look at the pinks and purples and read into them?

I'm glad you read into my colors. My hope is that color can ignite words into the photographs. I often think about poetry when formulating my

When I look at Mapplethorpe, I can only look at his work through what I take as his own ironic gaze. The relationship between flowers and femininity, the uptown, black smoke glass coffee tables, the European-money side of Studio 54 when the Warhol crowd moved their party to fancy apartments rather than the Factory studio. The old women who were friends with their hairdressers. Those images conjure up many things that I think you actually try and dismantle in your work. I wonder if it is outdated of me to think that the strength of the homosexual gaze is that it dismantles everything and then fuses it together with a new authority.

Funny, because I never actively thought about dismantling or re-mastering with a new authority. I think it occurred in my work out of necessity. I agree that the strength of the homosexual gaze is about dismantling and re-appropriating. At a certain point in my life it was as if

Overall, what I have always found satisfying in your work is a sense that you really like photography, rather than use photography to talk about what you really like.

I am in love with photography in its purest, original sense. I do have issues with the associations made around the tightly wound medium and often anal, process-oriented photographers, but I'm still very interested in the true magic of light, film and chemistry.

I would like to remain a purist with photography and push color with the alchemy of the darkroom, rather than using the two-dimensional process of a computer. The colors that emerge in the darkroom inhabit their own physical space, something you can't engage with on a screen. But I do use photography to talk about what I like. I love nature and people, the crust of the earth and shifting shapes, and these elements repeat in my photographs. You chose what to shoot and then you make another choice, in the darkroom, how to phrase it, what temperament to give it, depending on what color palette you design. I remember reading Ansel Adams' books about the negative and the print. I knew ahead of time that I would never master it, but I was intrigued that indeed, a photo could be many things depending on how it was manipulated in the dark.

I can't help think of Adams when I see some of your landscapes. In fact, it was only after years and years of looking at German landscape photography that I was able to dig that moon hanging over the desertscape in his famous *Moonrise, Hernandez, New Mexico* 1941.

In a critique at Yale, you once asked if I consider myself a romantic. I didn't understand the question fully then, but it lingers in my head. I answered in a literal sense, saying that I am a romantic in life, which I wore as a badge of honor in grad school.

I still consider myself a romantic, though I think my recent pictures talk about a more universal romanticism, nature often being an emphasis. Ansel Adams is probably the most universally known photographer because the power of his work is the power of nature, which we all feel yet have trouble articulating. When traveling through American landscapes for my work, I think of the romanticized Ansel Adams, trekking high and low, waking to the sunrise and having a notion of a higher power and just being humbled by our place in the world. His photographs are so much about beauty and majesty, but it's a nostalgic beauty recorded in black and white photography. I started printing in saturated colors as I was bored with the standard "correct" color balance taught in college. I had to express that higher feeling of being privy to the extreme power of nature, and I tried to translate it through color.

When I was in elementary school we watched a sci-fi movie in the auditorium. It was projected, so it felt like we were in a theater especially set up for us. The film was about a mirror planet where everything was the same, but everything on the left was now on the right. An astronaut lands on the planet and thinks he is home, but things seem just slightly off. As soon as I let go of my own fears and said goodbye to the straight lie I was living, some time in my mid-twenties, my world seemed to mirror that film. My work opened up in such vast ways when I came out, but everything in my life had to be reconsidered. This new understanding led me to realize that nothing was in its "right" place because the idea of a "right place" is fictional. And I always return to that sci-fi film and think about moving around in a life that seems practically yours but internally you know that it doesn't belong to you. I think both of us make works that at times allude to a past in which we had to practice until we came to our present. The homosexual gaze can be seen to devour both what responds to us and also, that which does not even notice us. The works are multi-sided and related to worlds that look similar but feel quite different.

The film sounds like a perfect metaphor. For the most part, I feel alien to the external world I live in and its society. We didn't create the past but we're stuck in the past's present. If I ever feel that things are in their "right" place, I push myself to create disorder and chaos because it's is just a more conducive way for me to cope with the world. Genesis P-Orridge speaks of fighting the numbness of being content. It is easy and natural to feel content, but more interesting to create discontent. That's the reason I make art. We create comfortable spaces for ourselves to exist in, but I think that comes from our fear of instability, our fear of something new. I want to see something new, to shed new internal light on these conditioned exteriorized worlds that we present to each other.

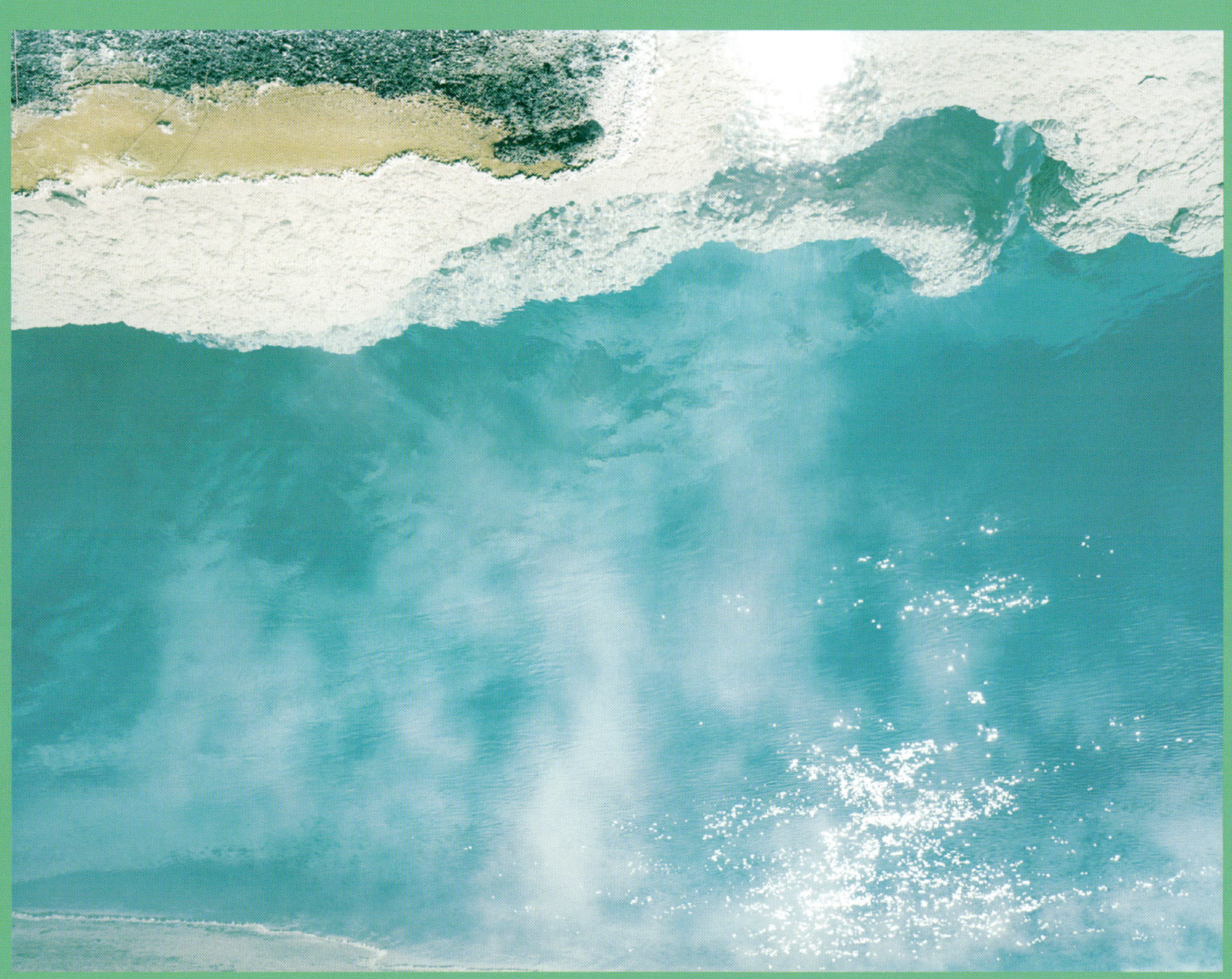

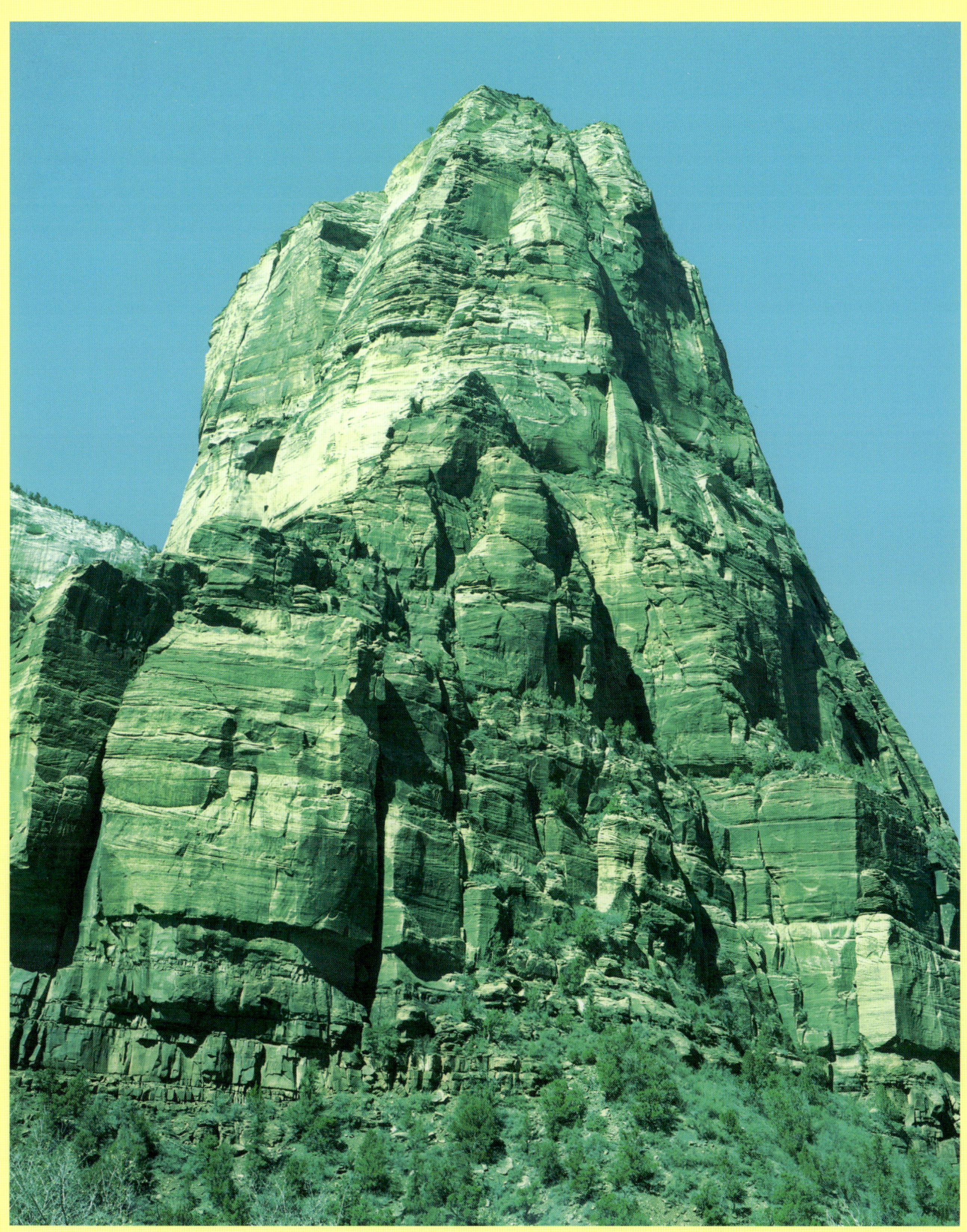

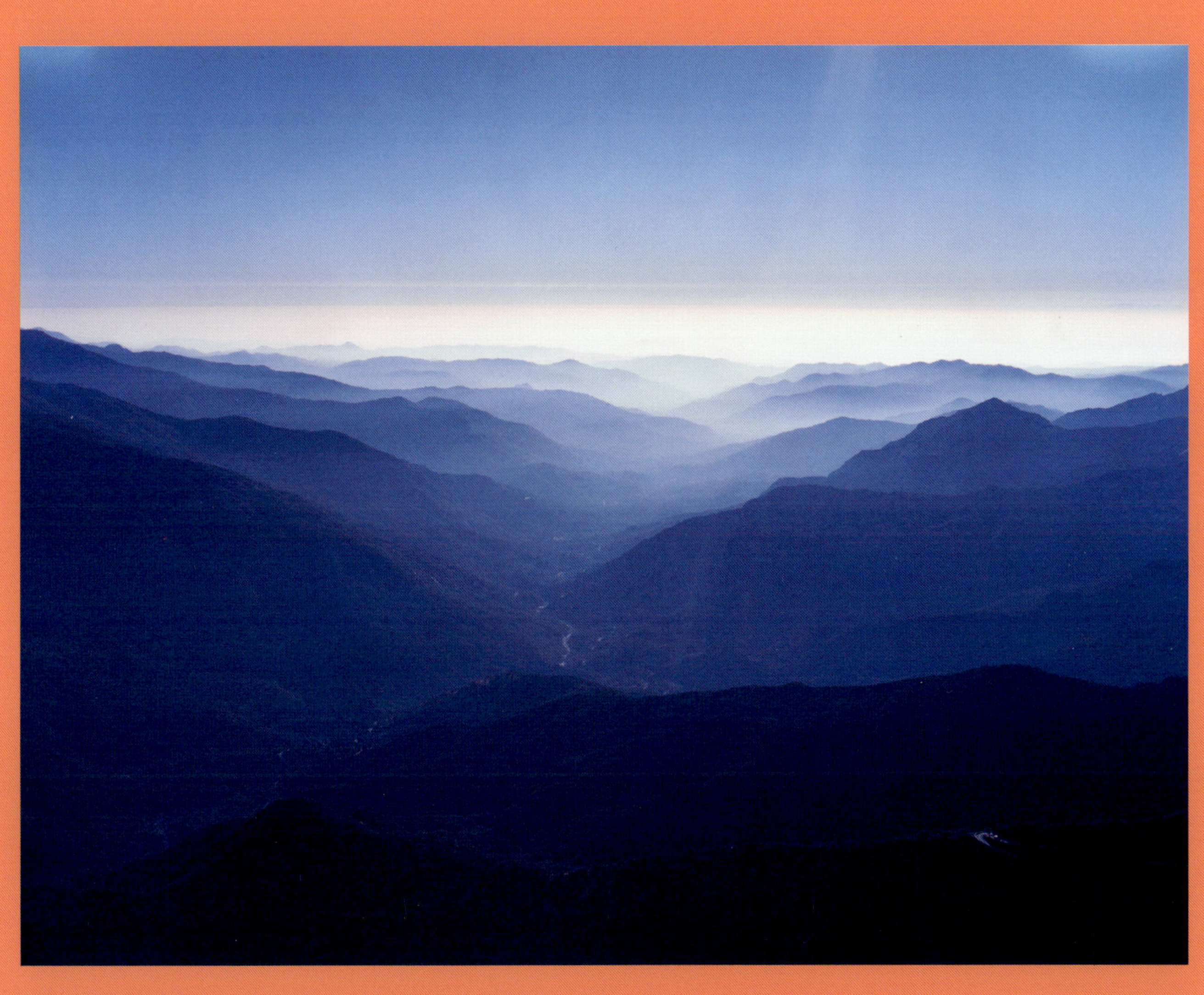

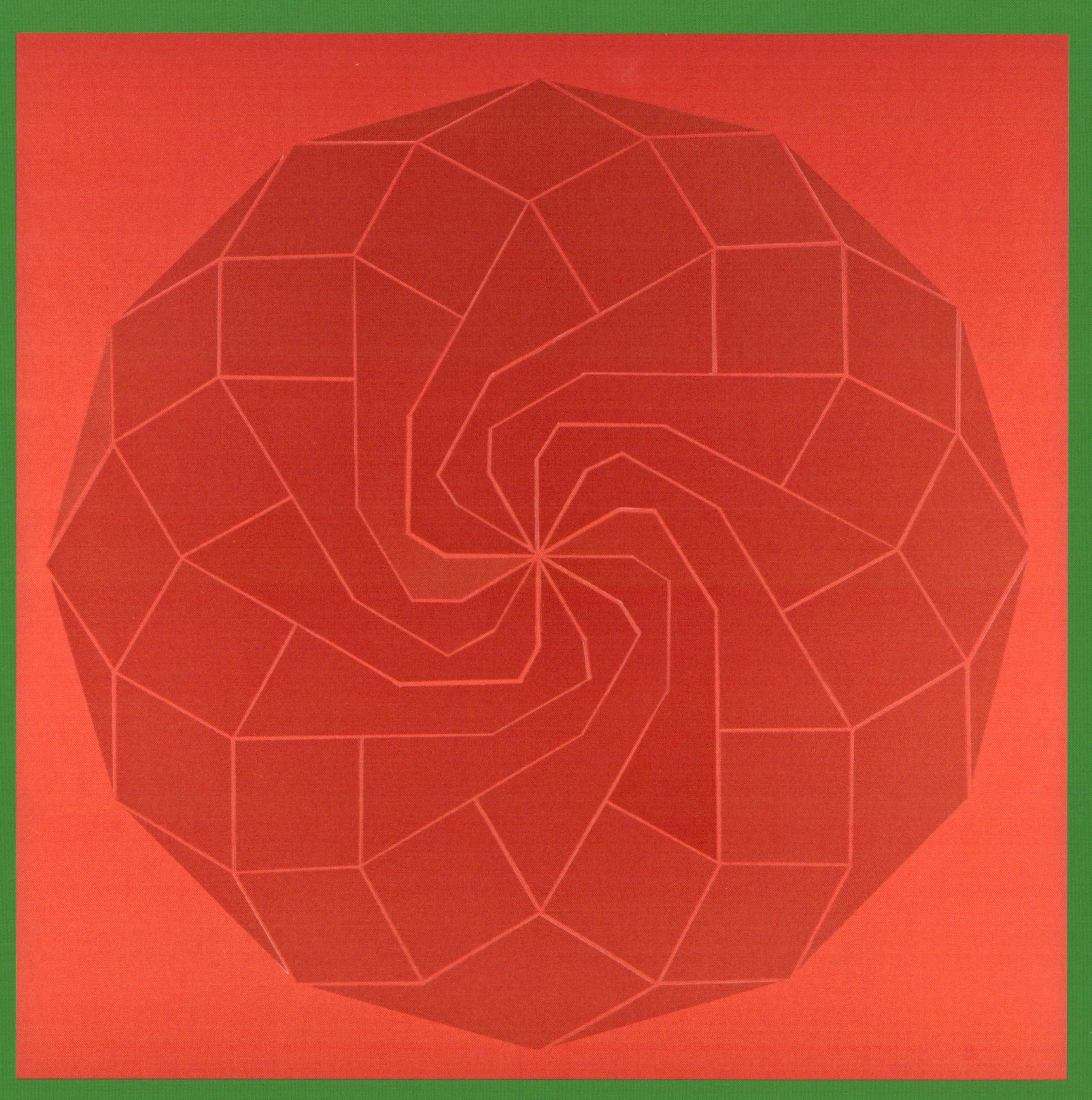

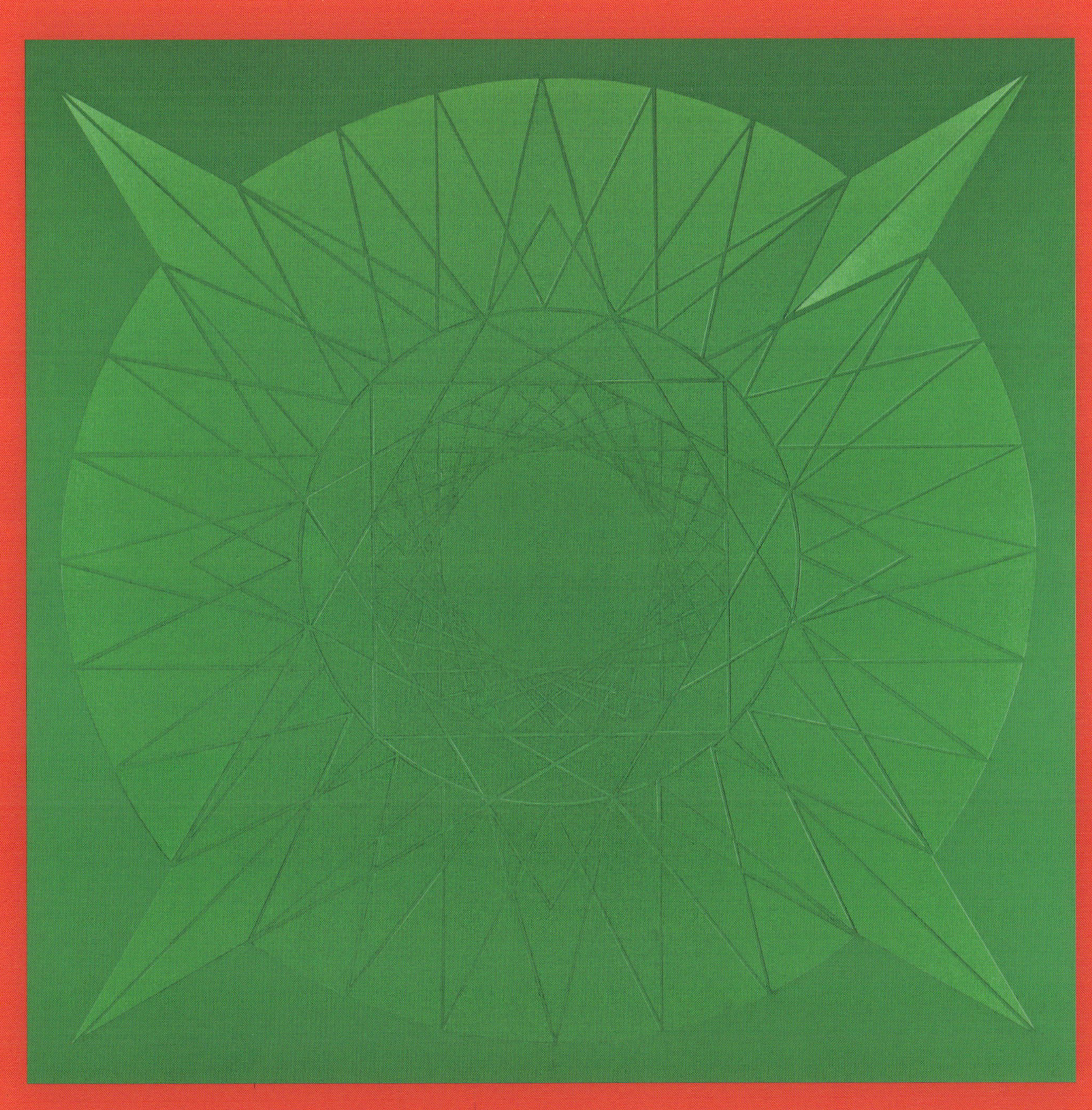

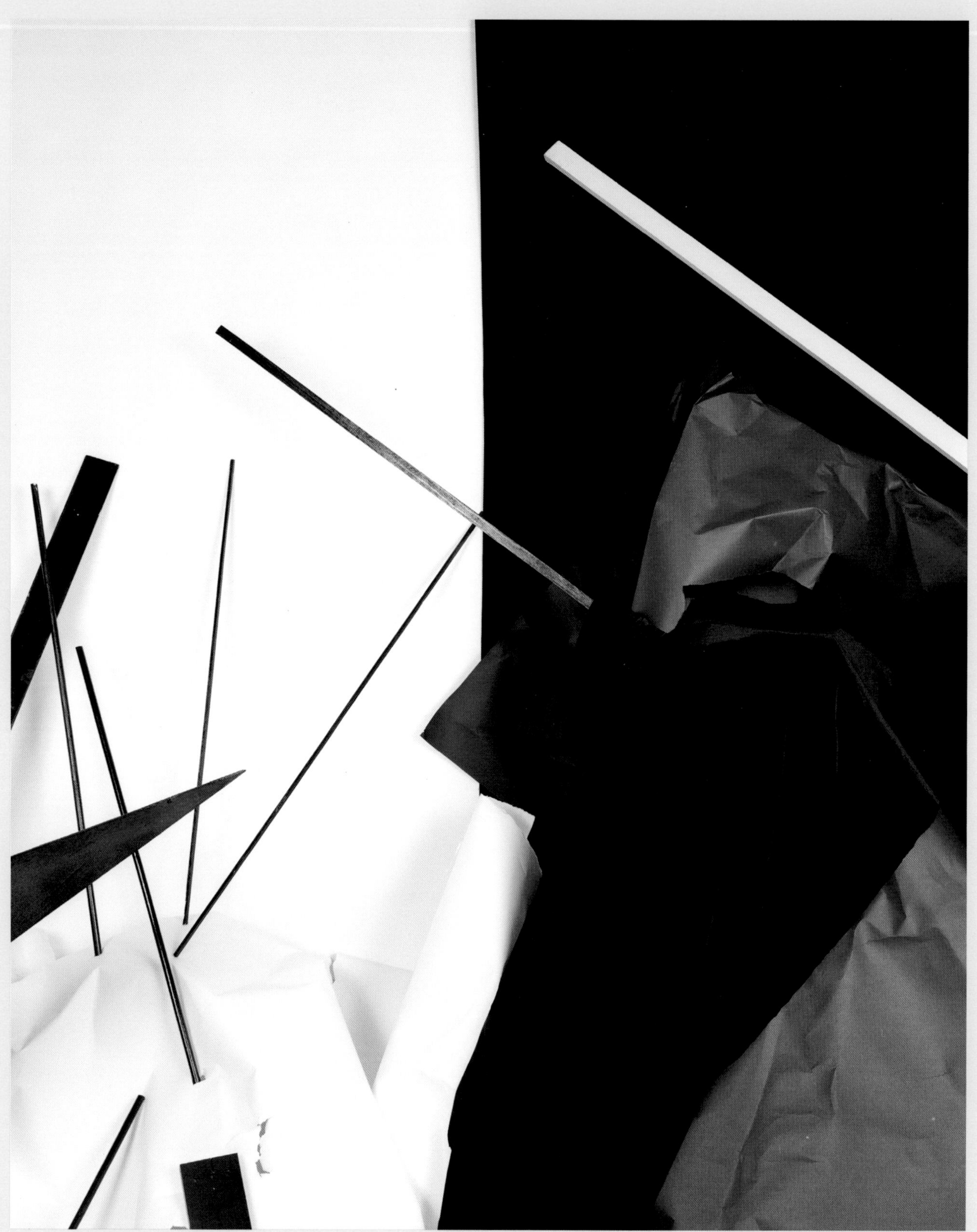

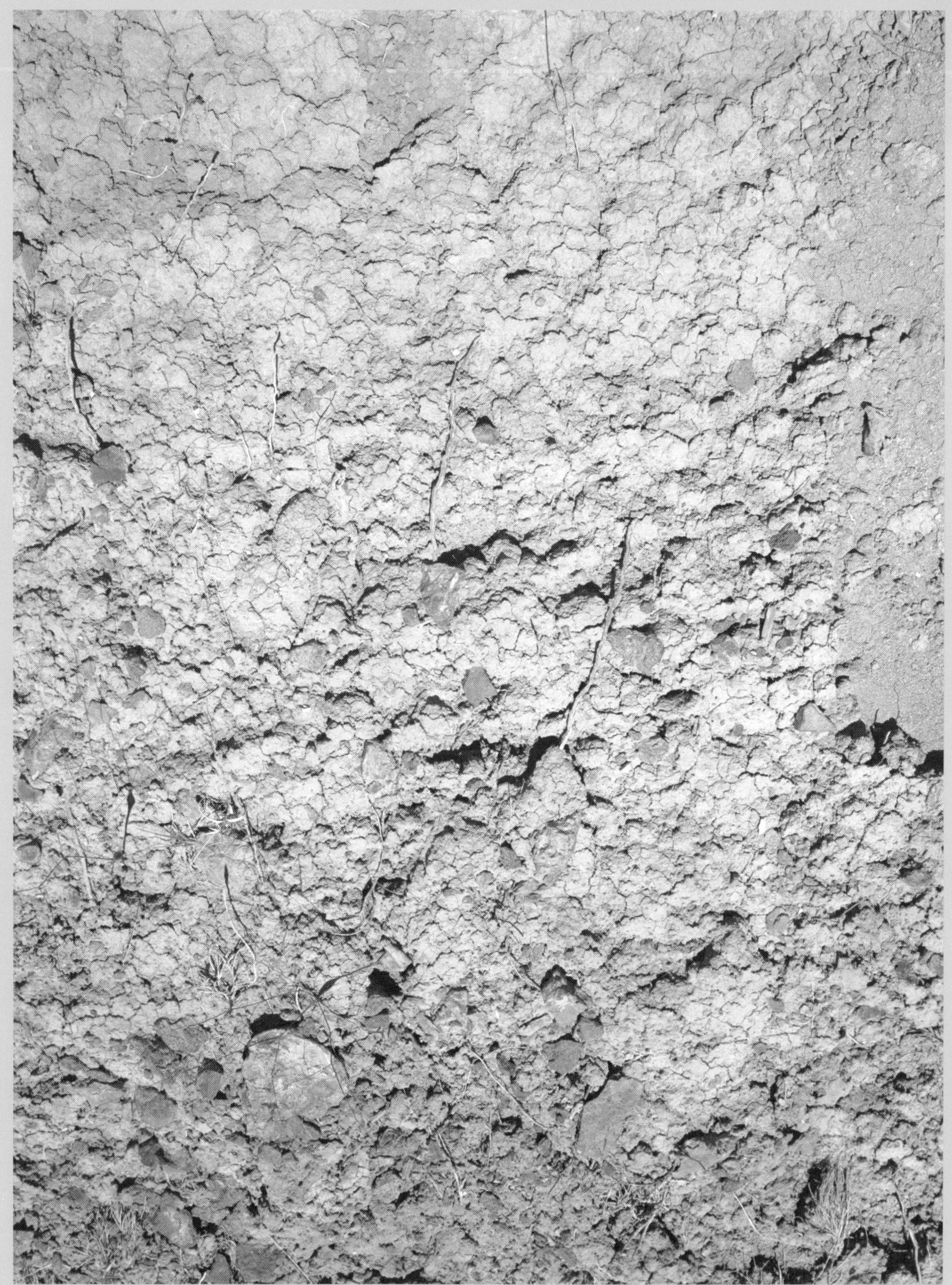

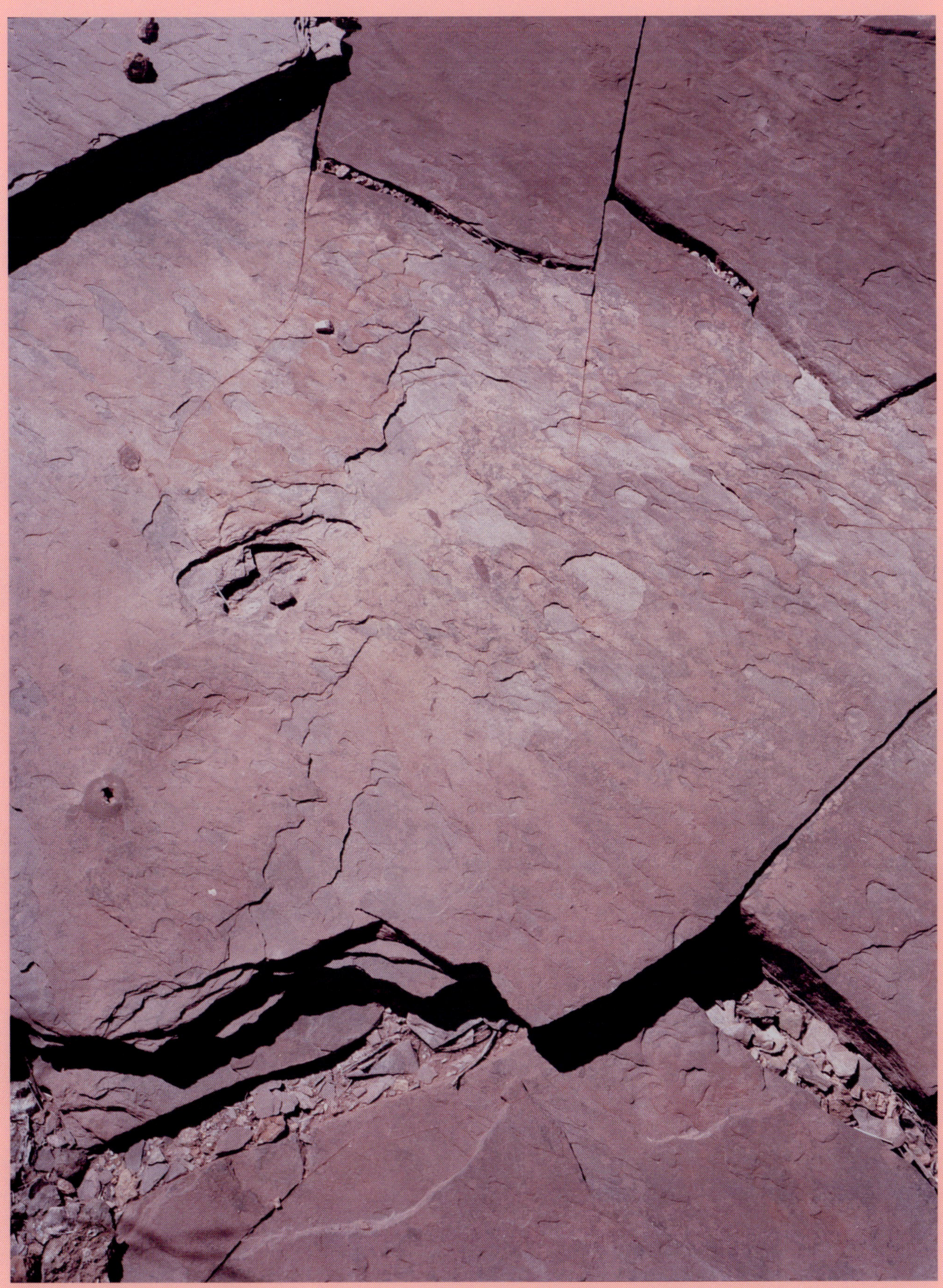

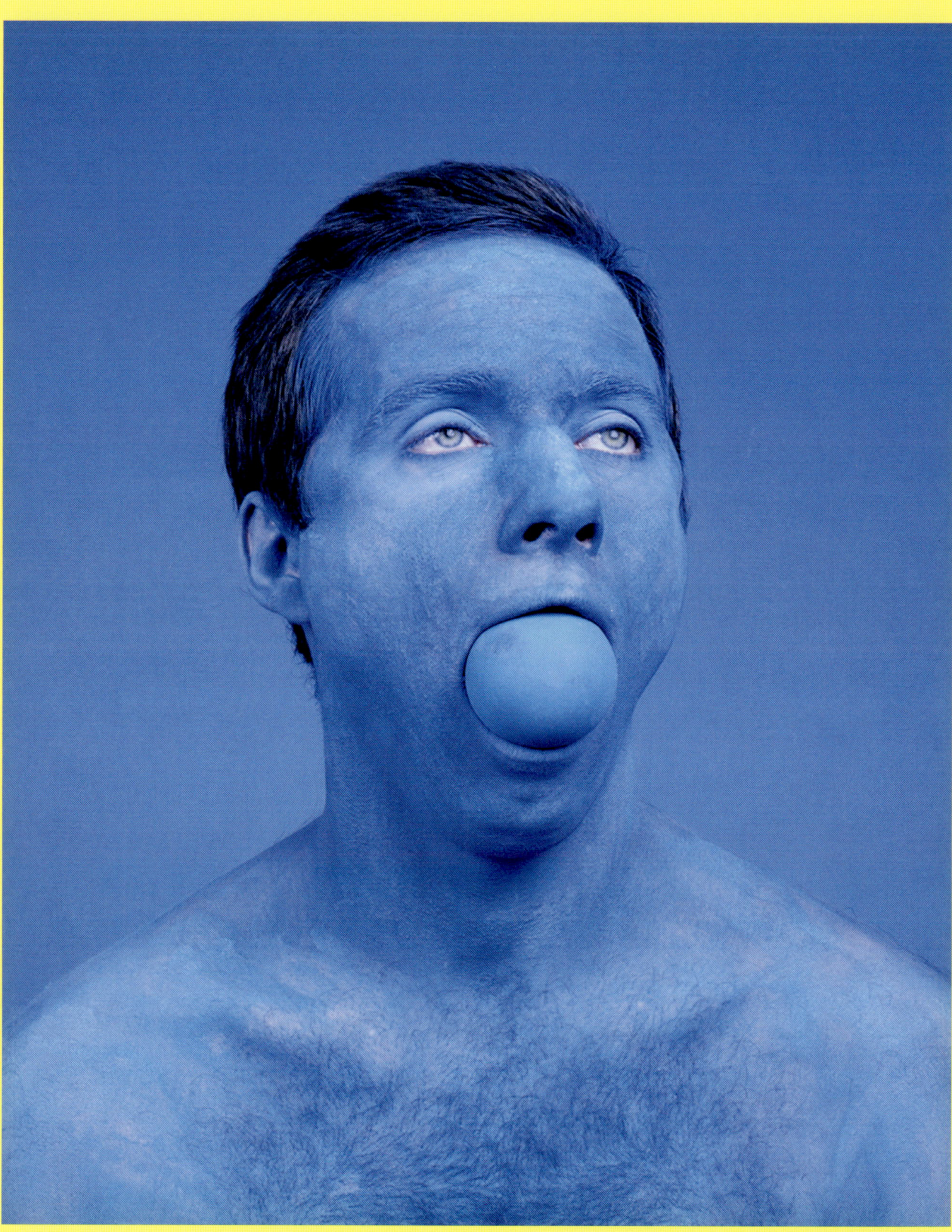

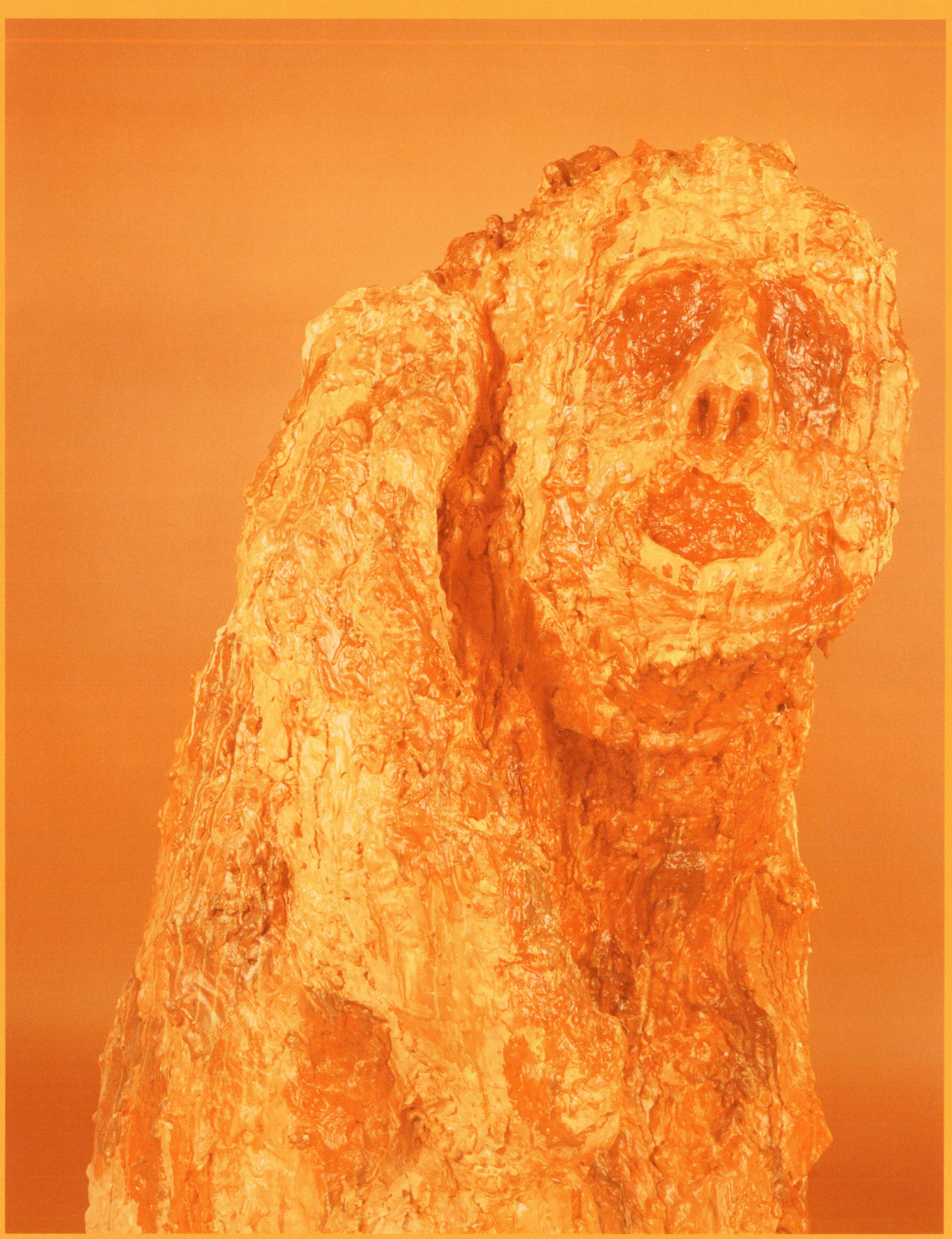

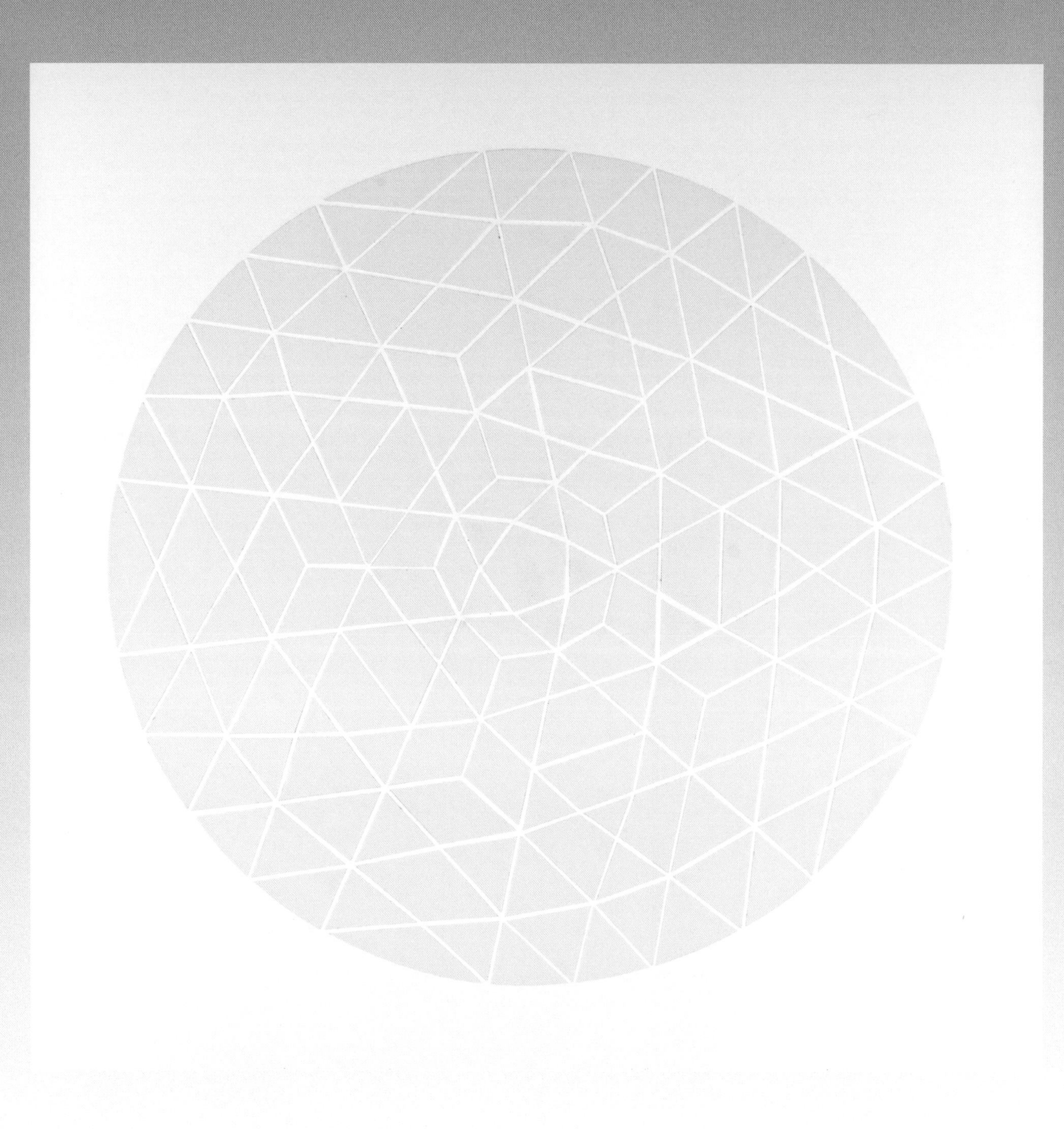

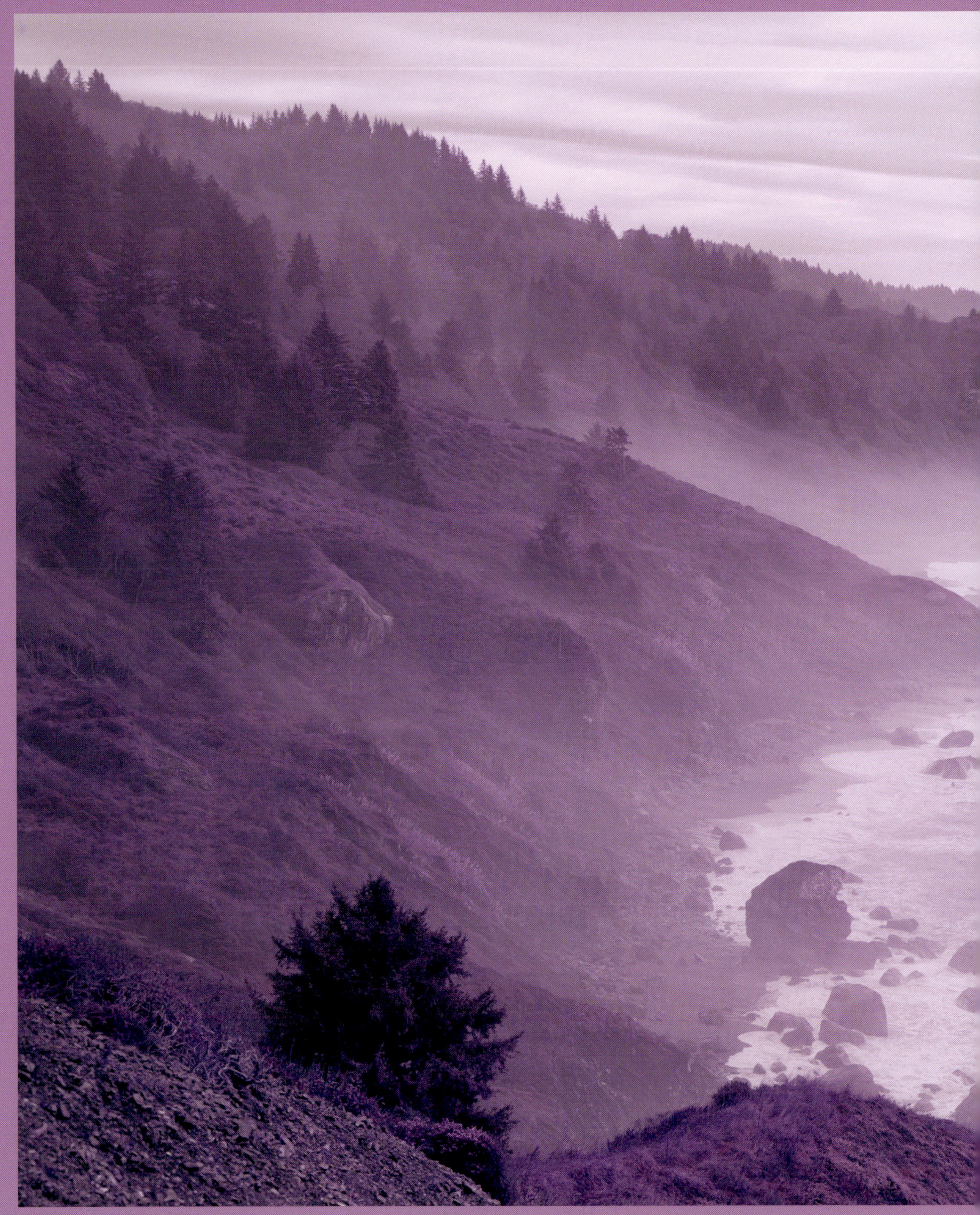

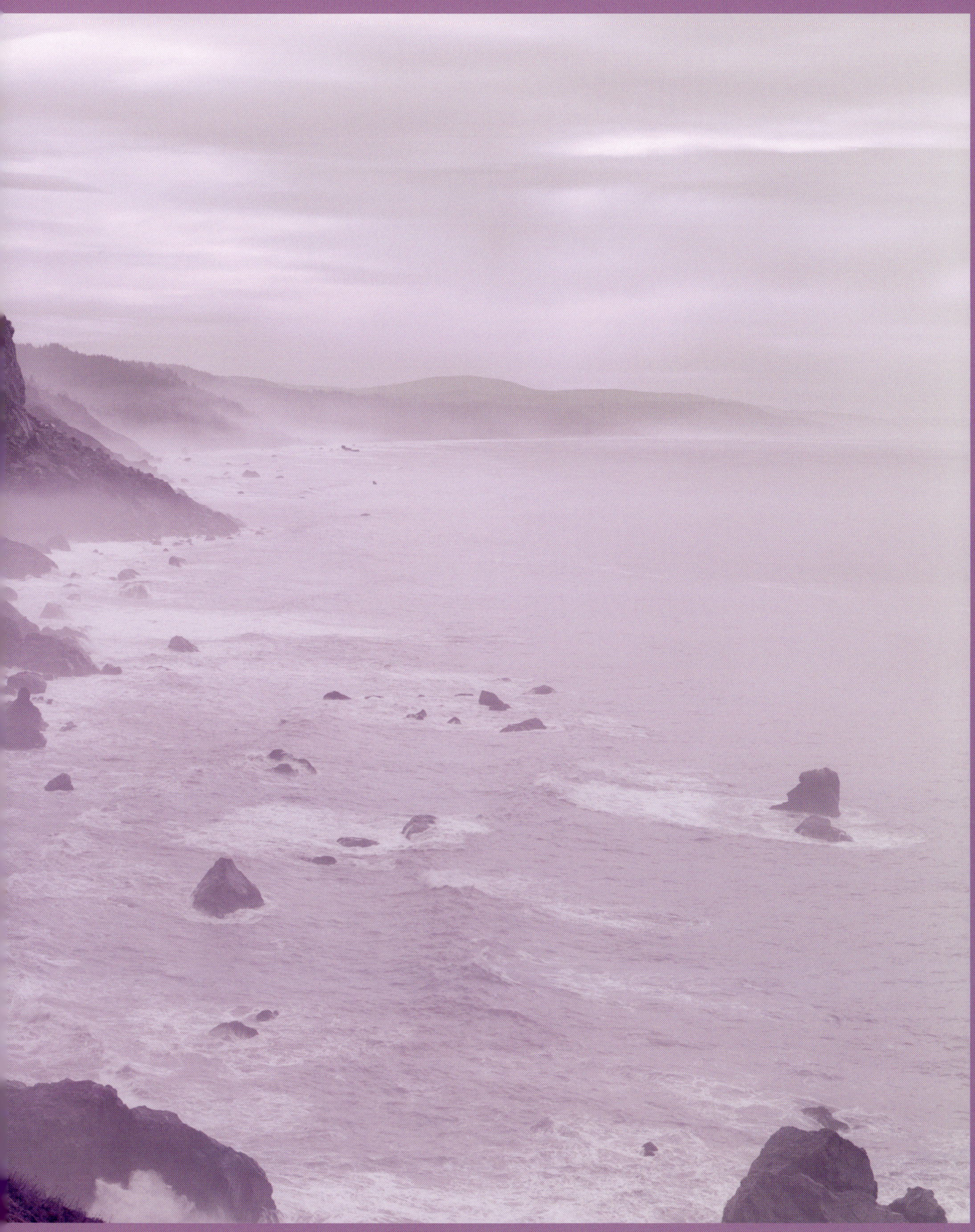

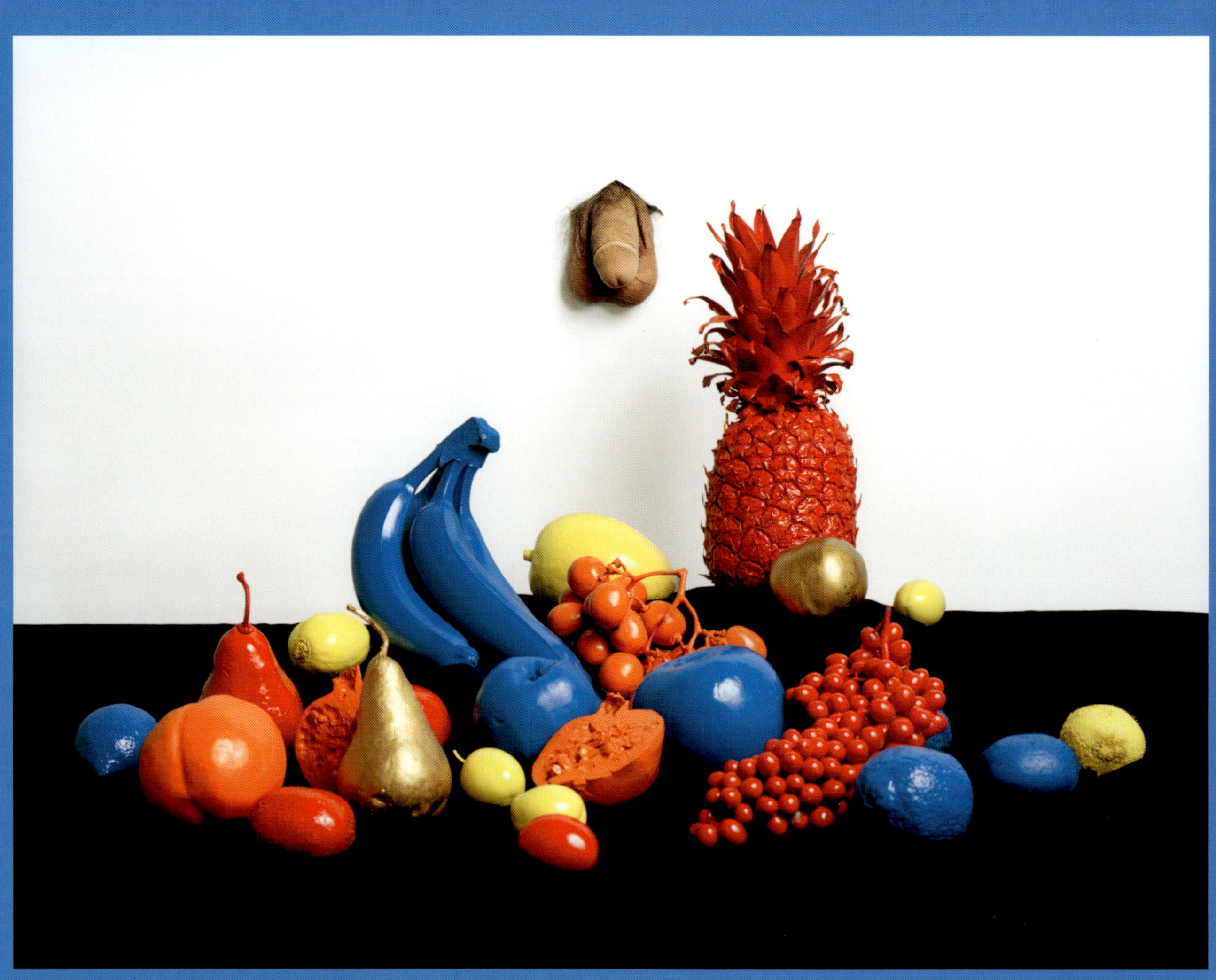

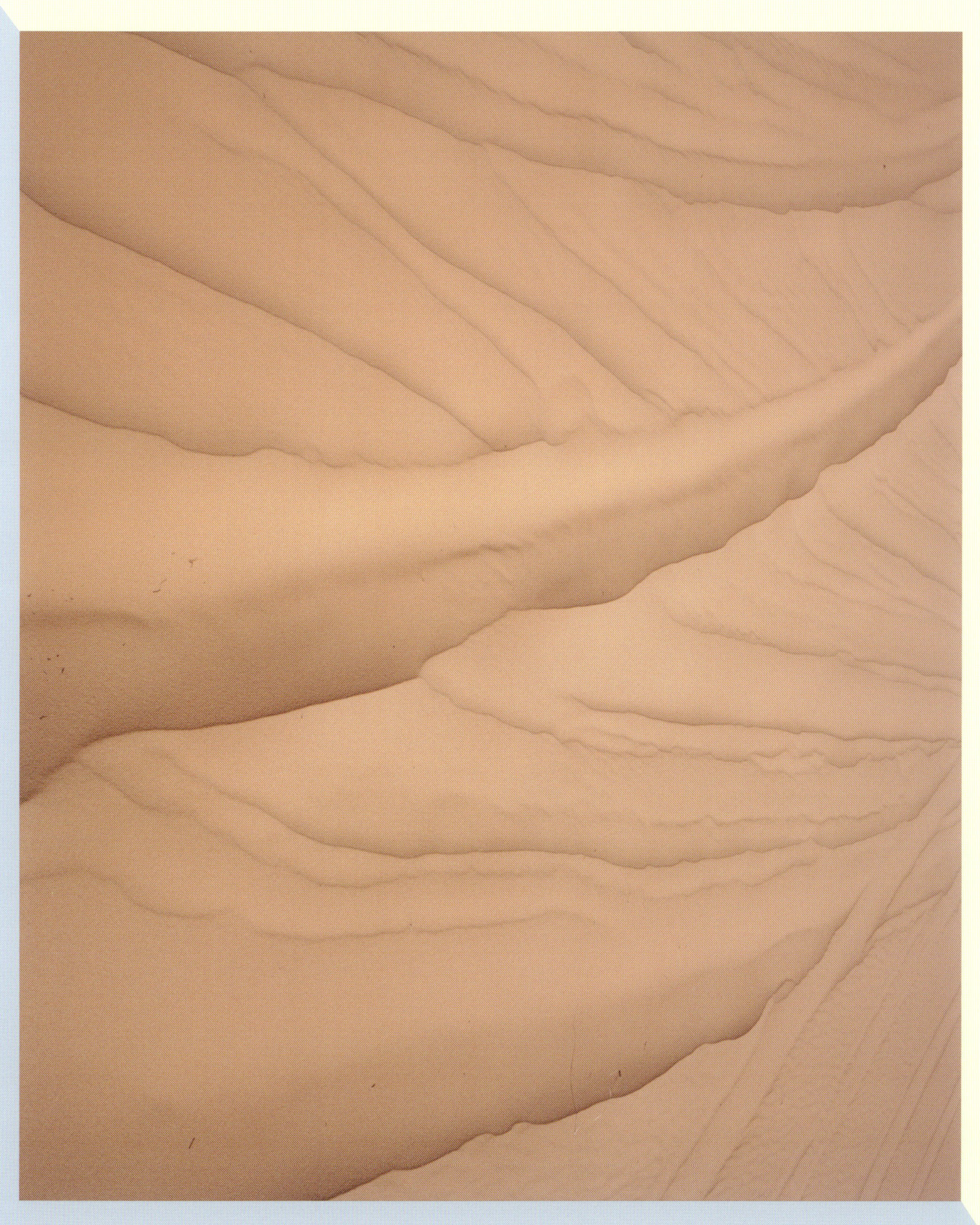

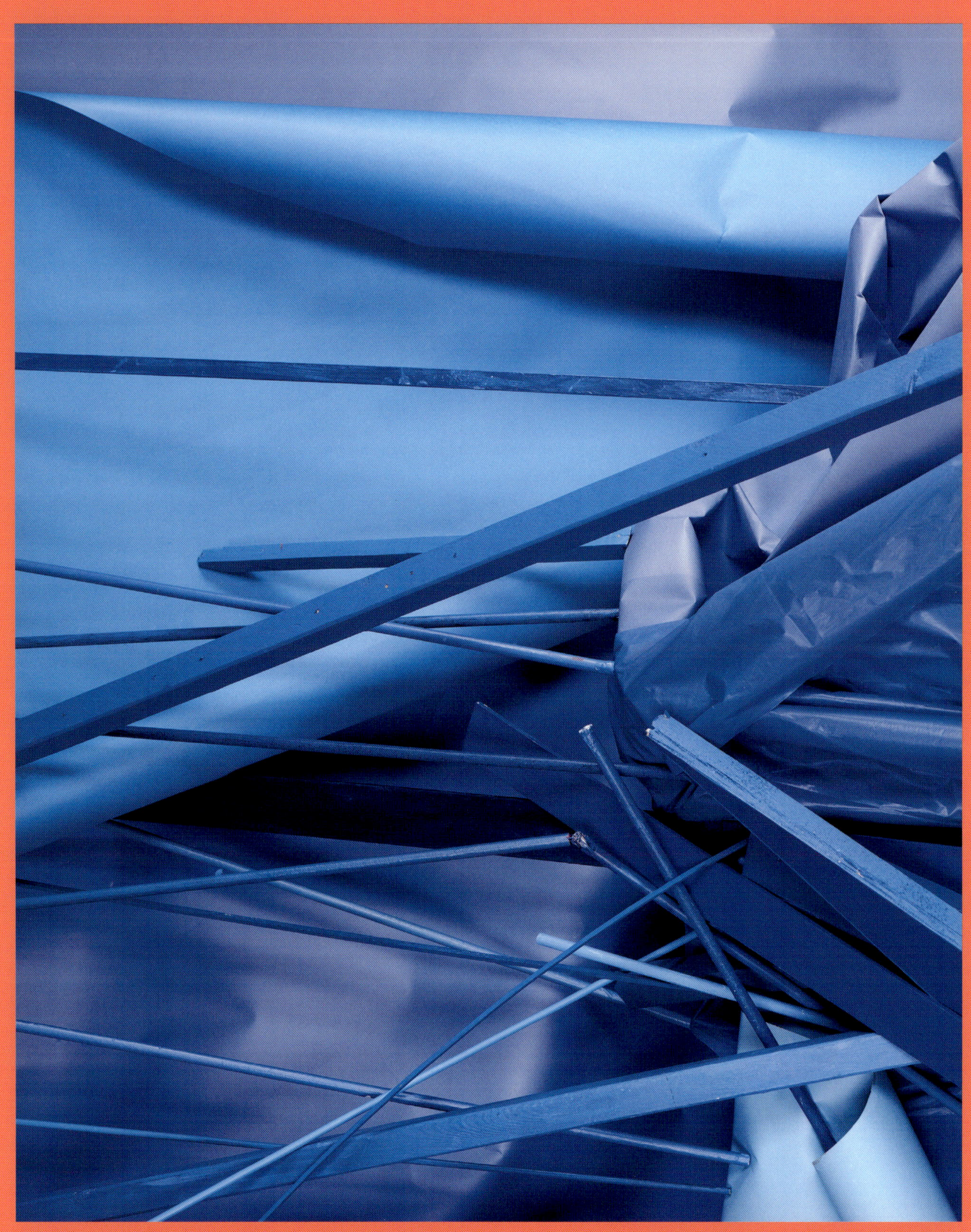

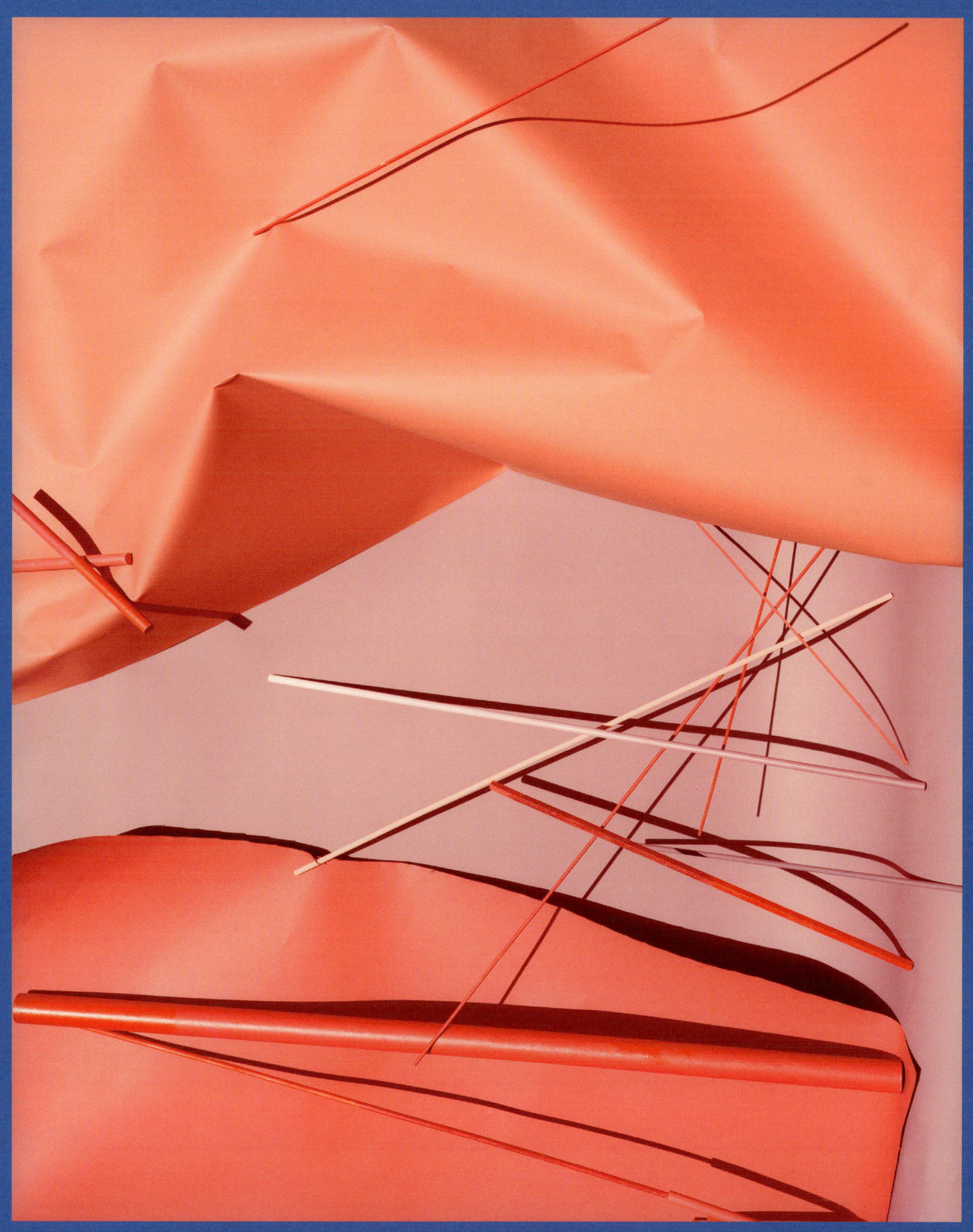

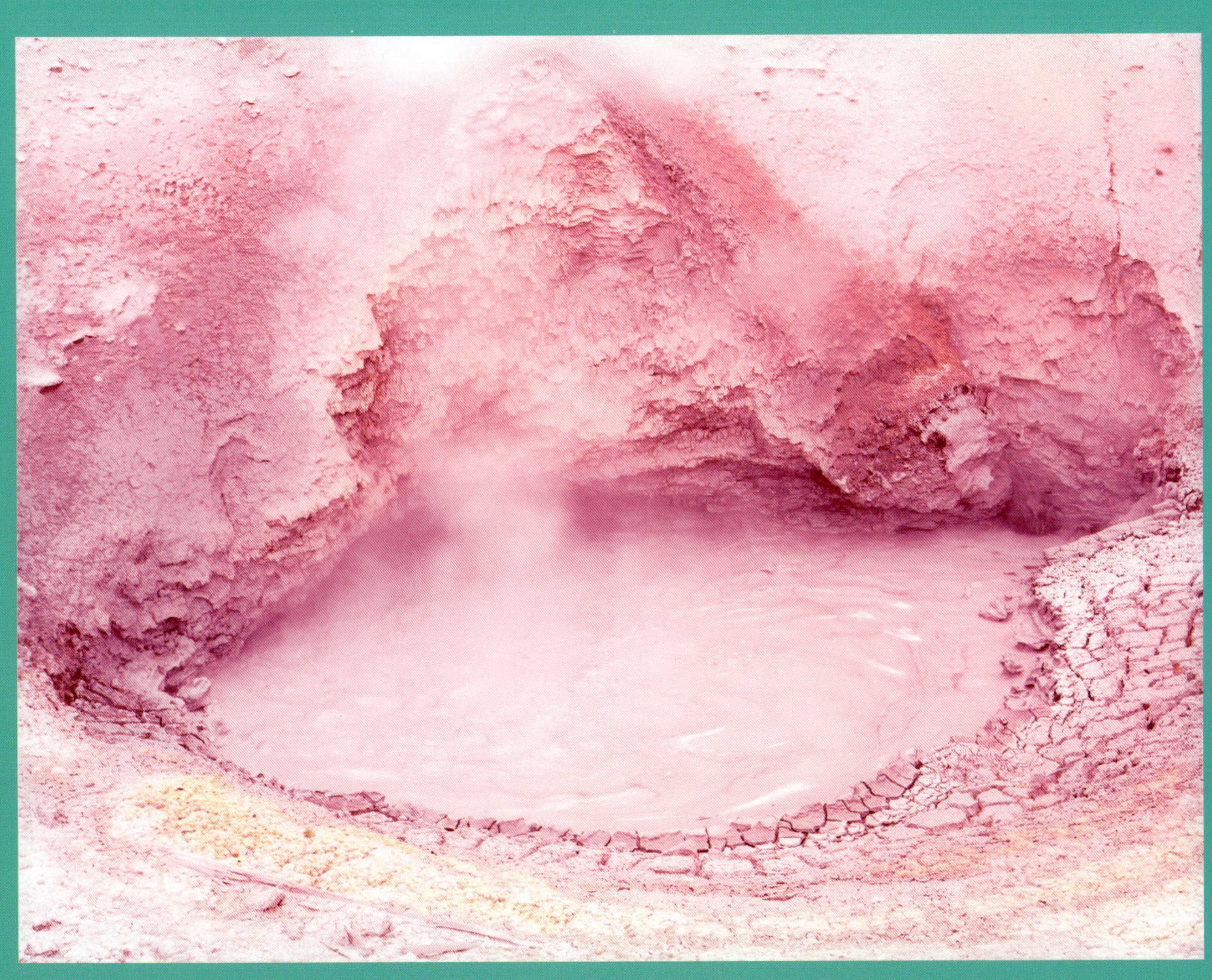

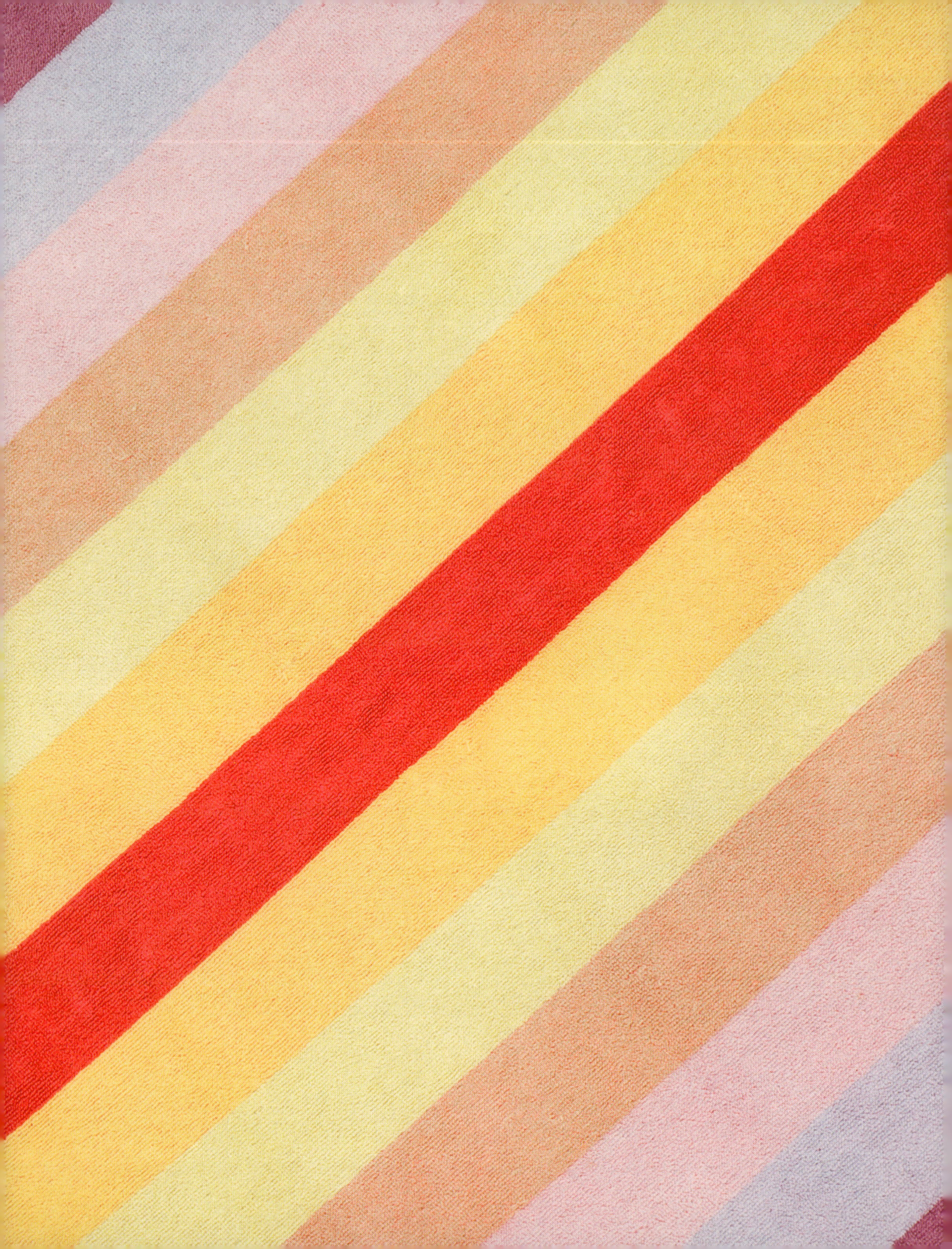

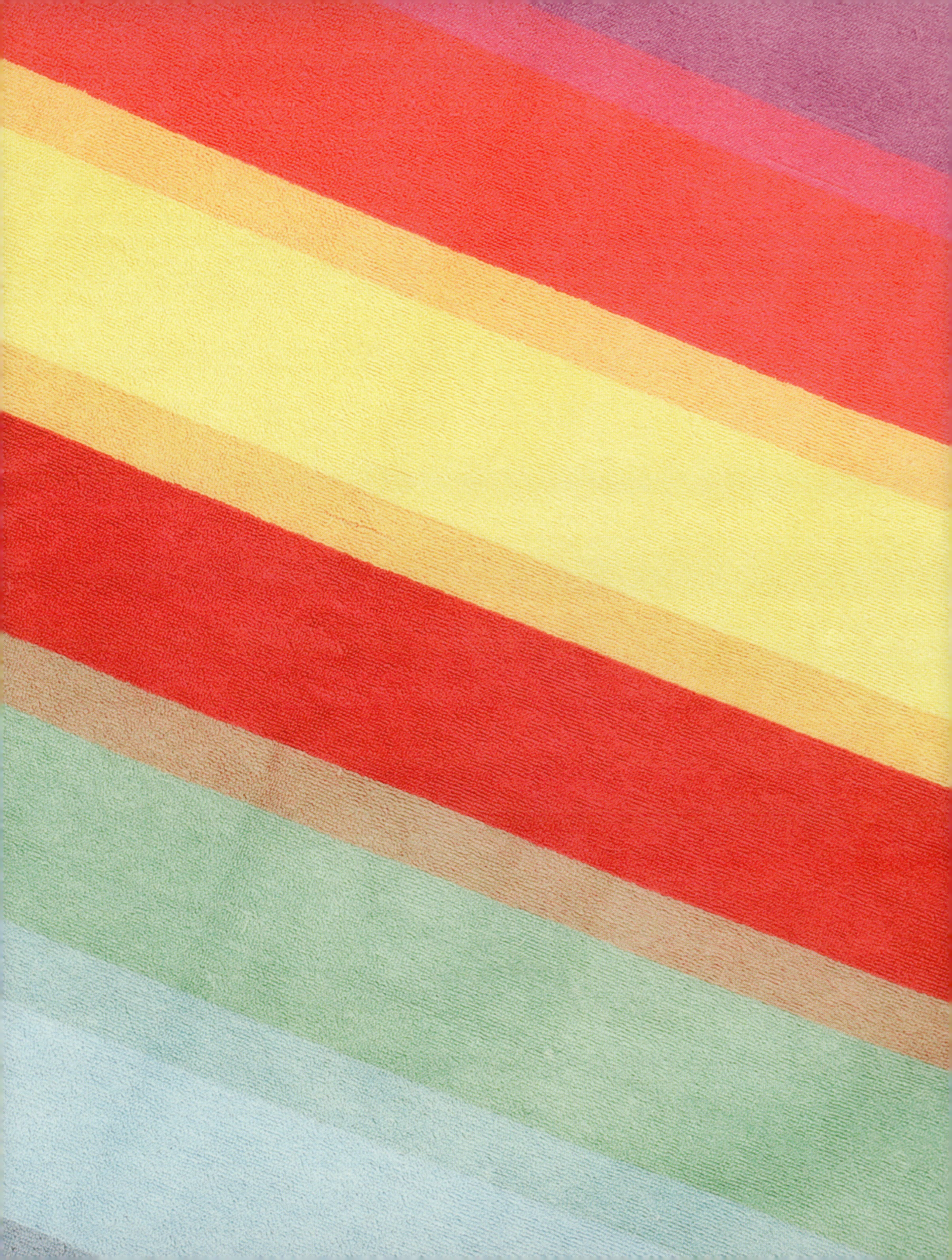

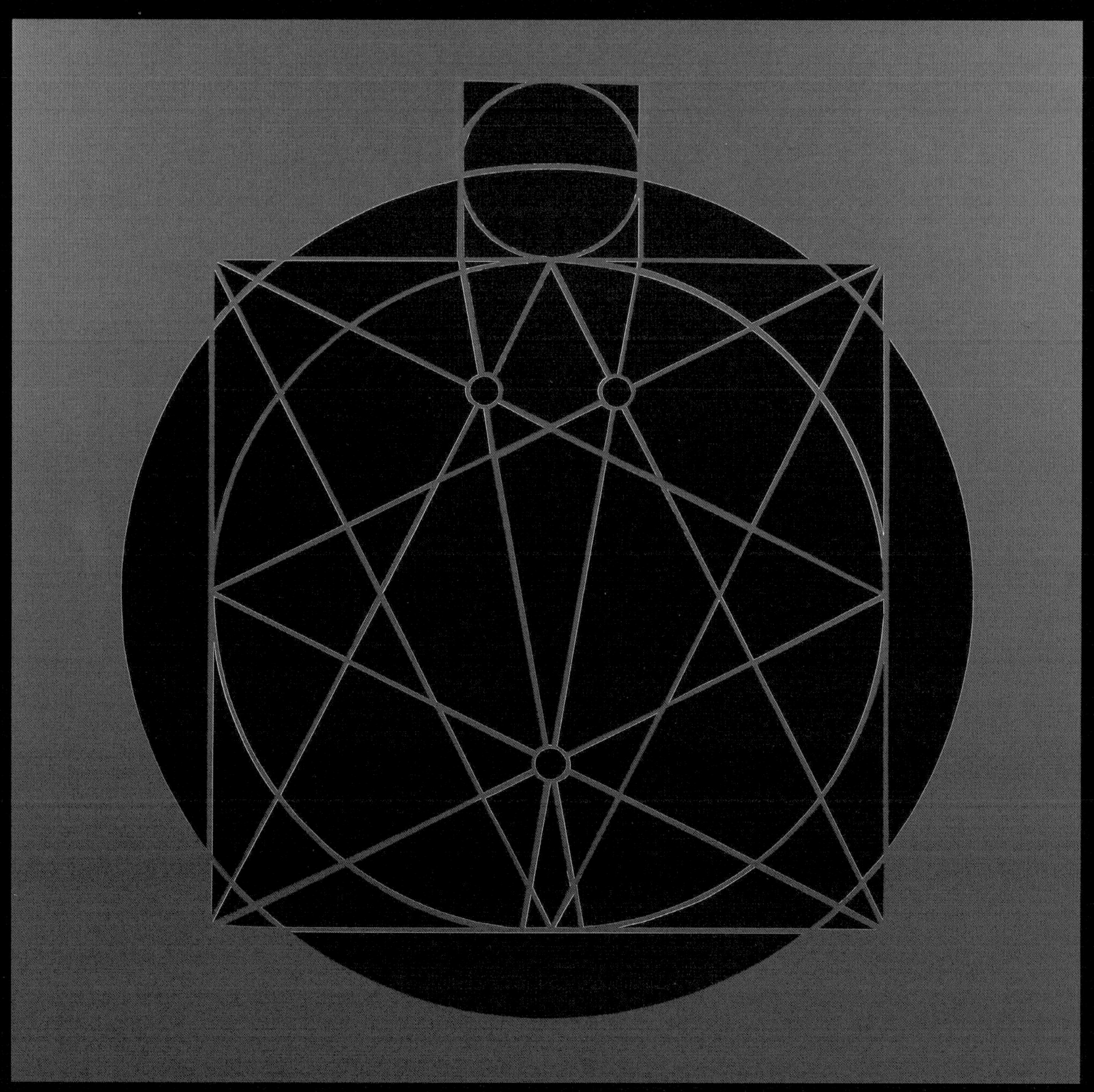

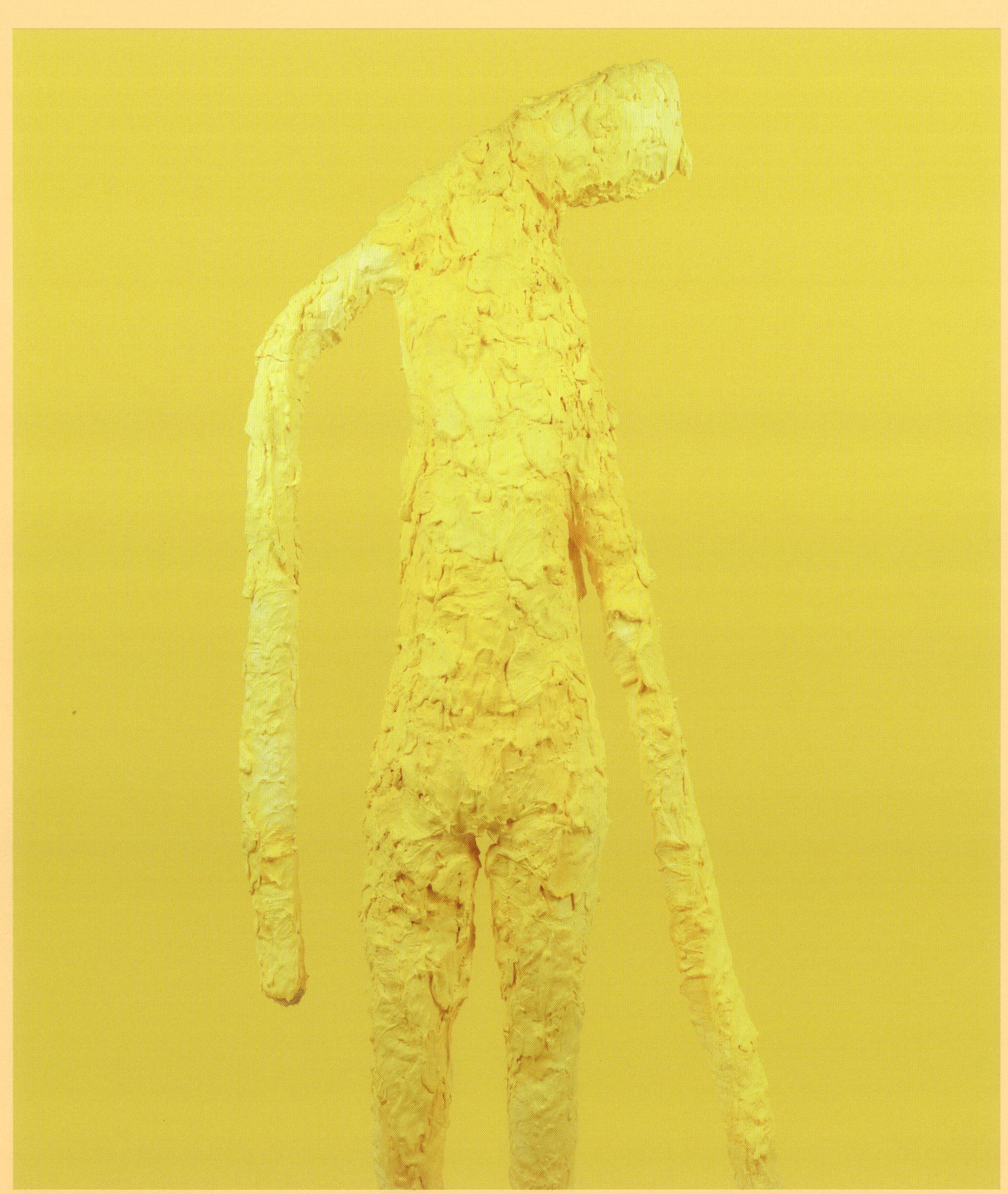

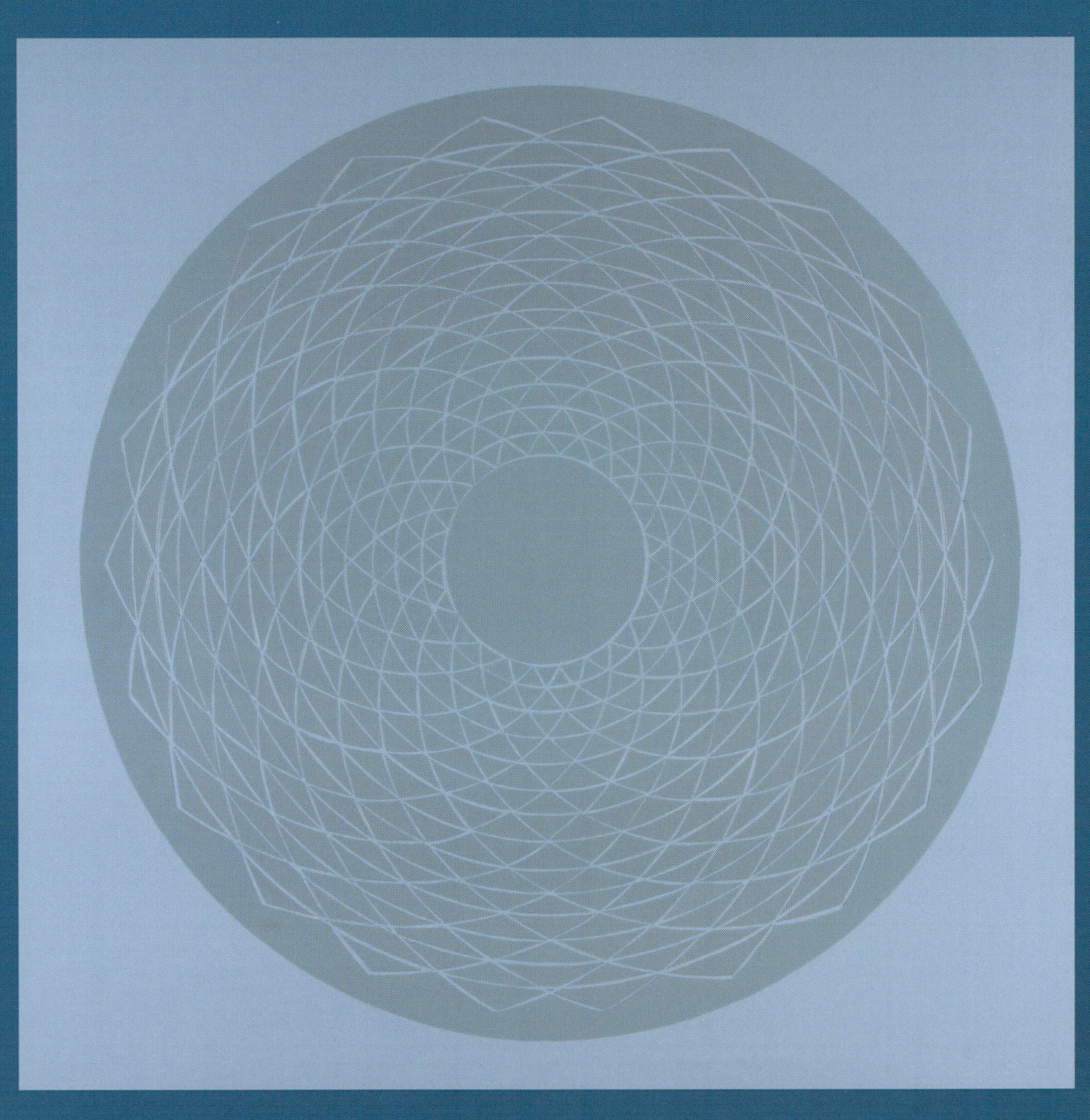

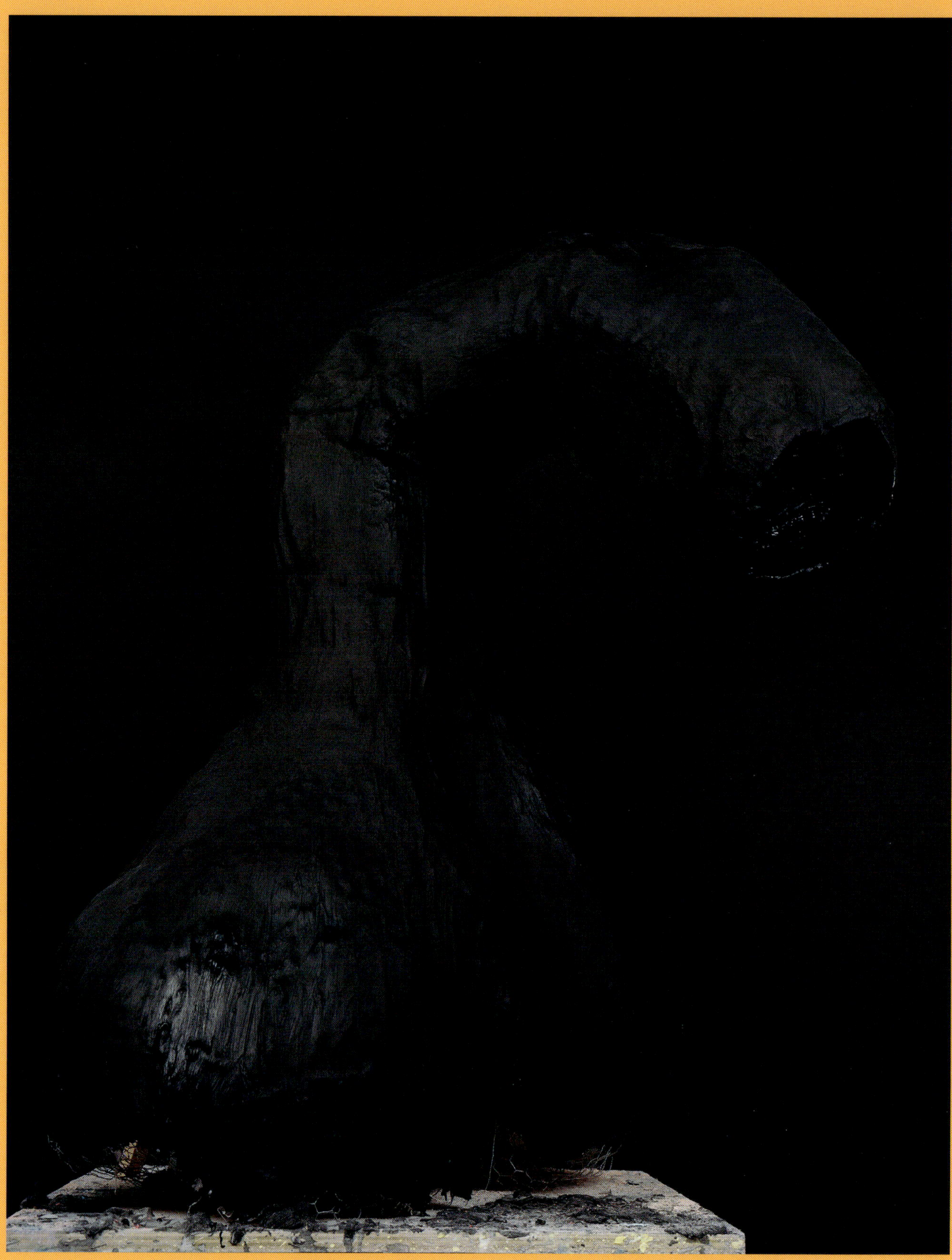

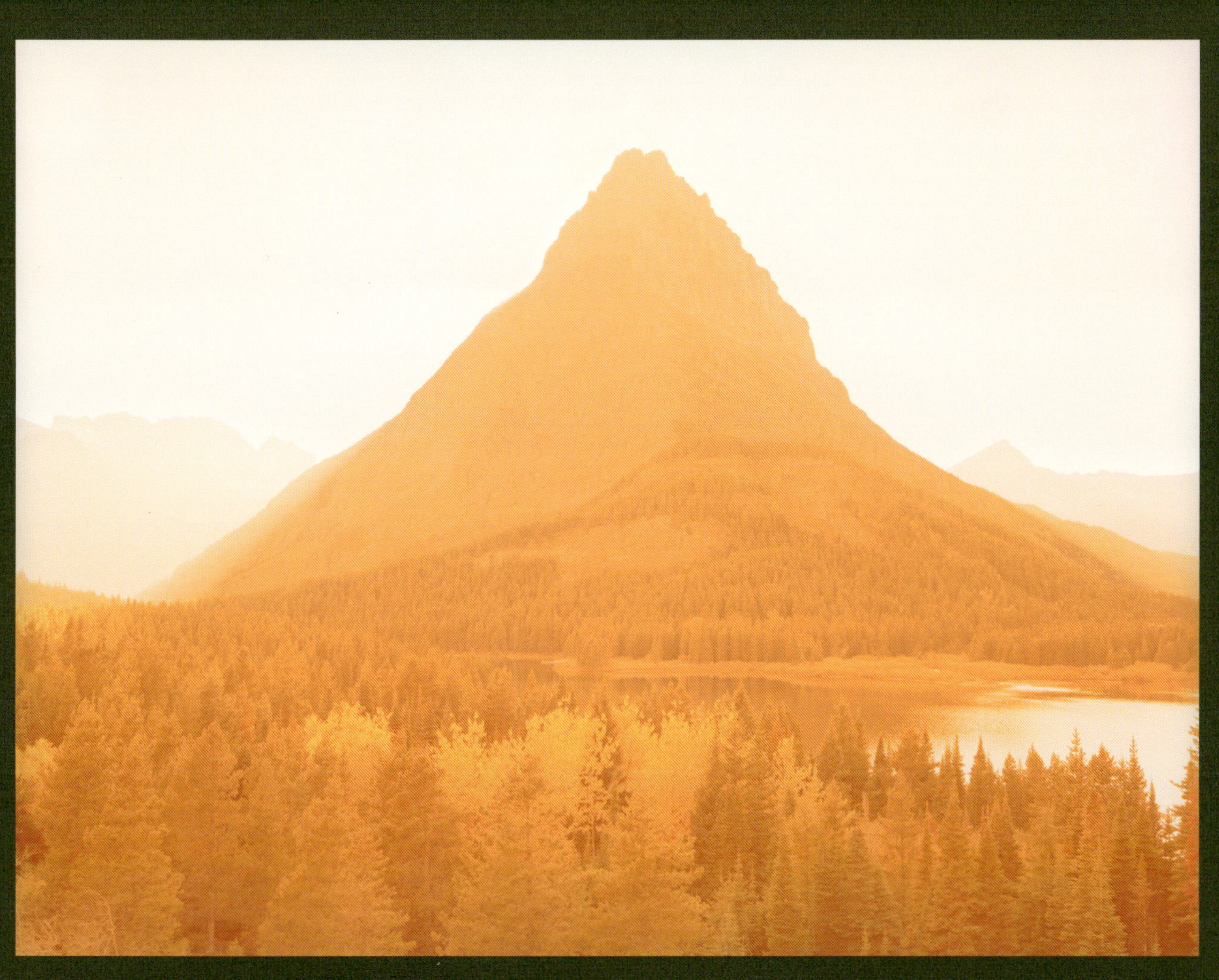

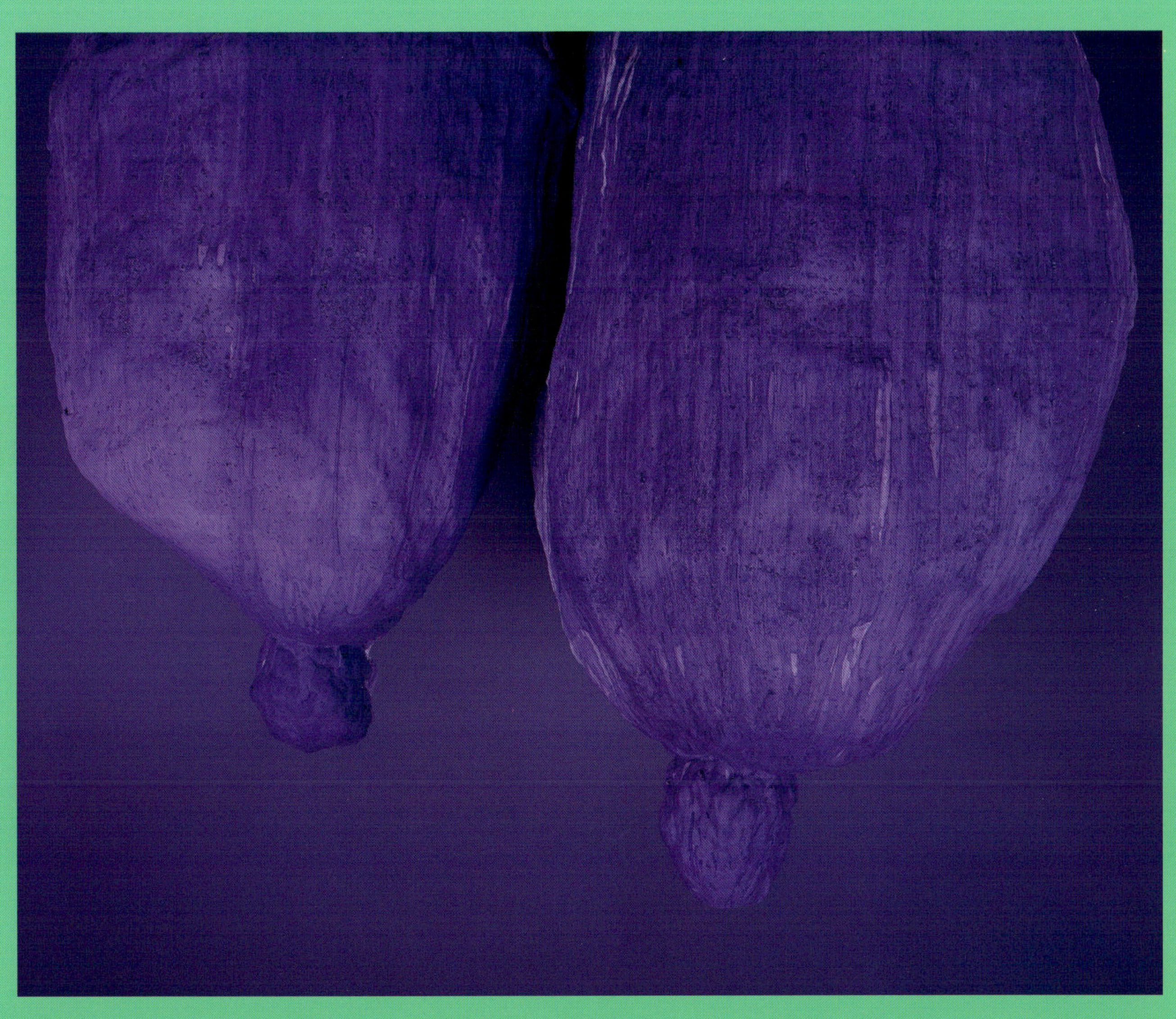

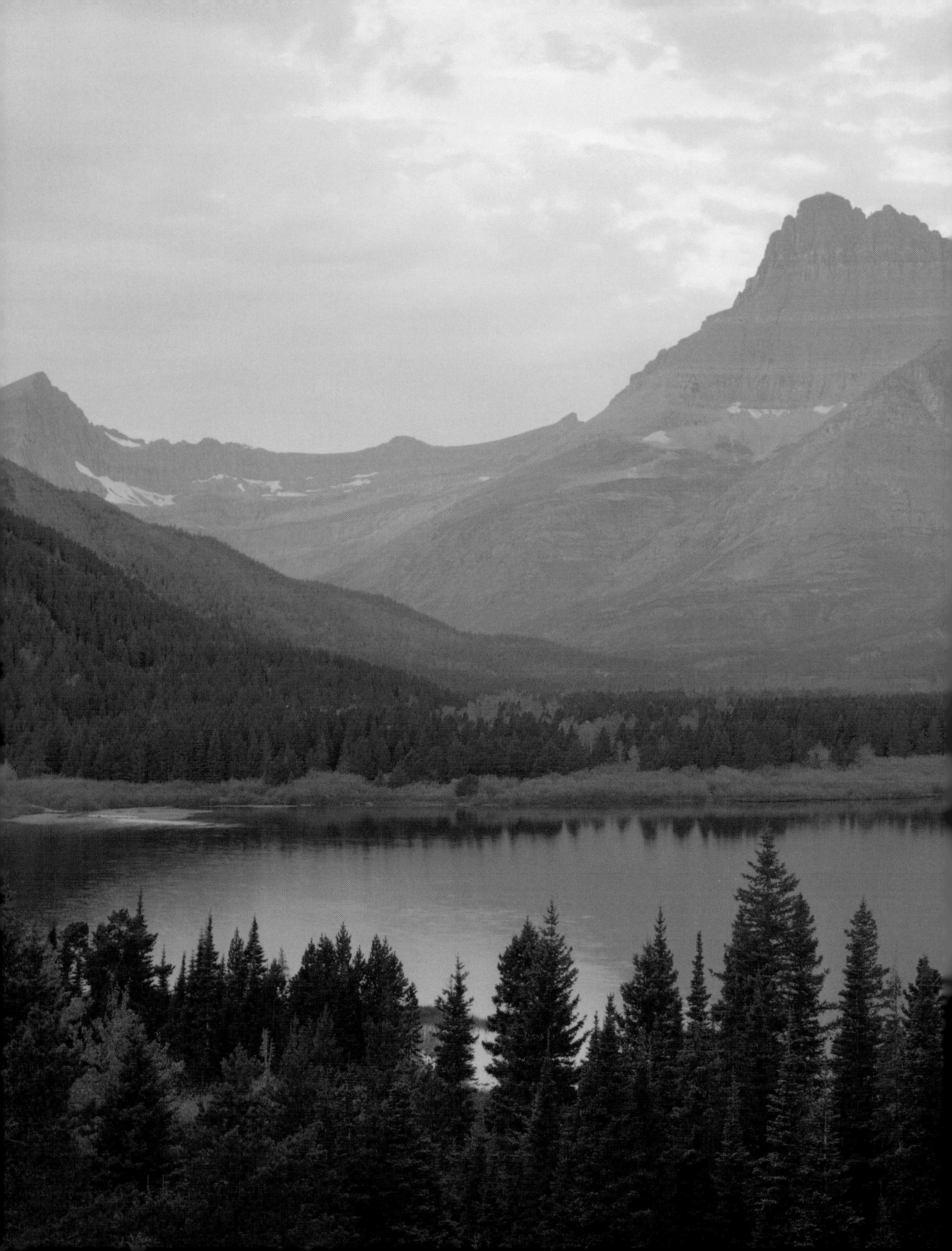

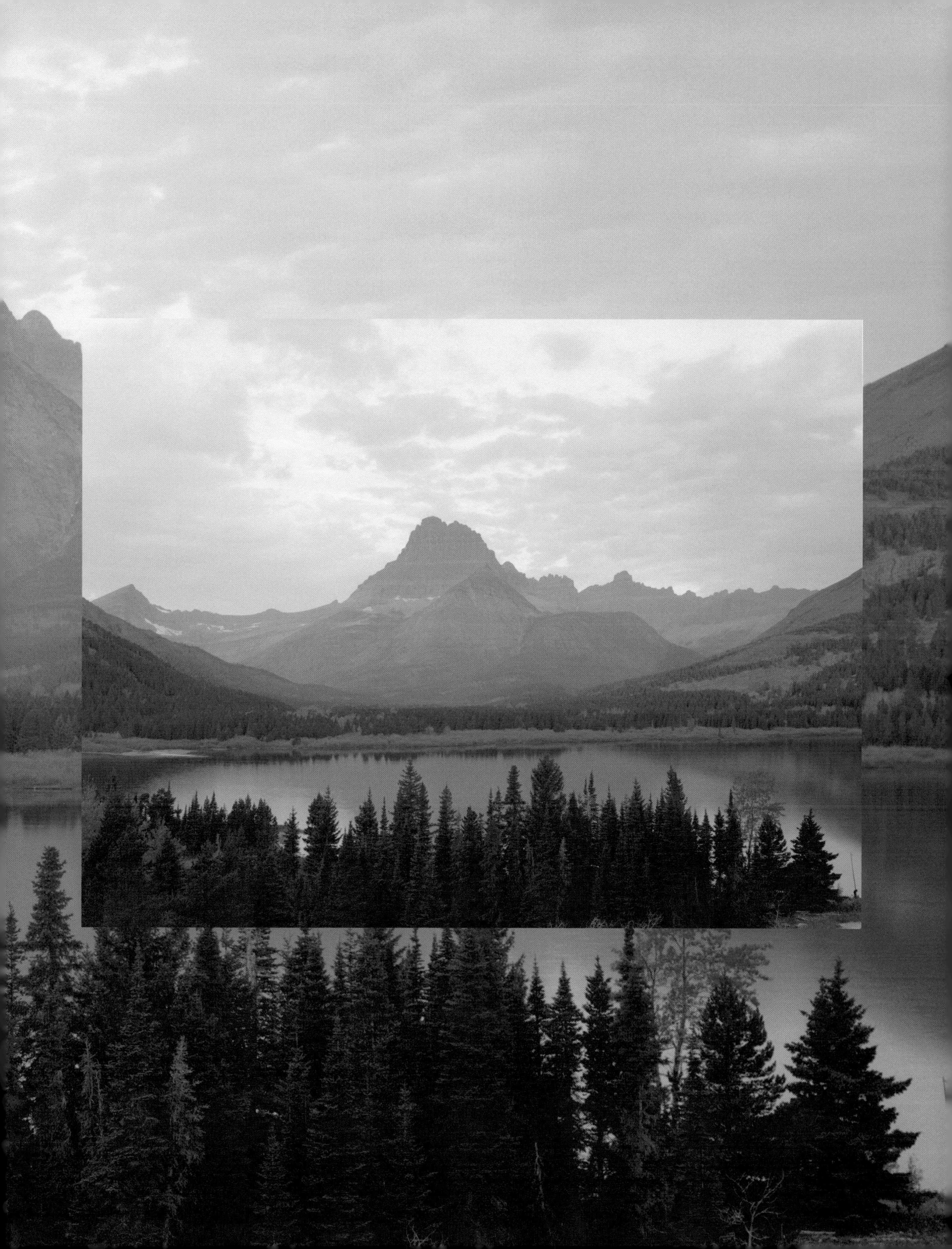

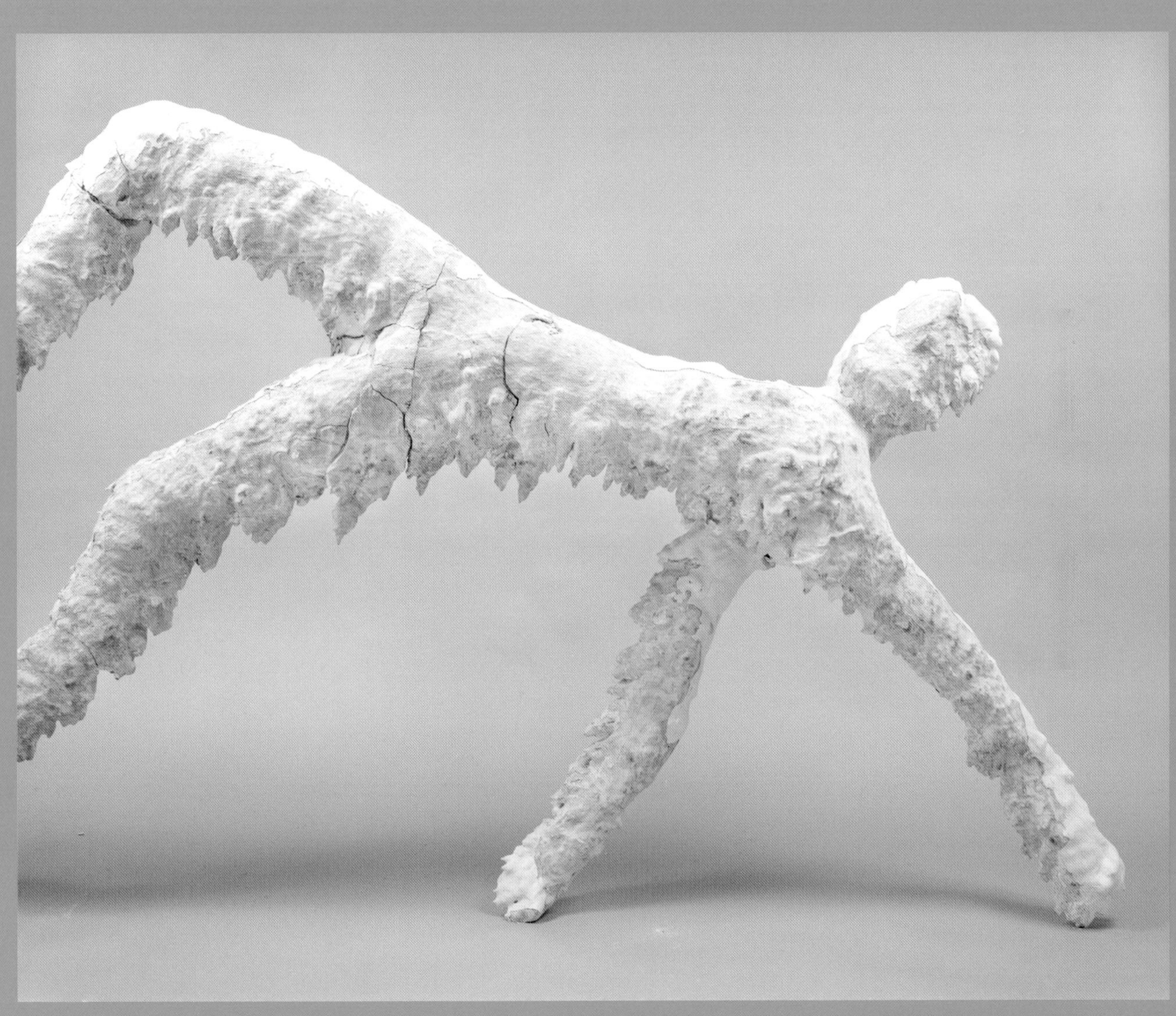

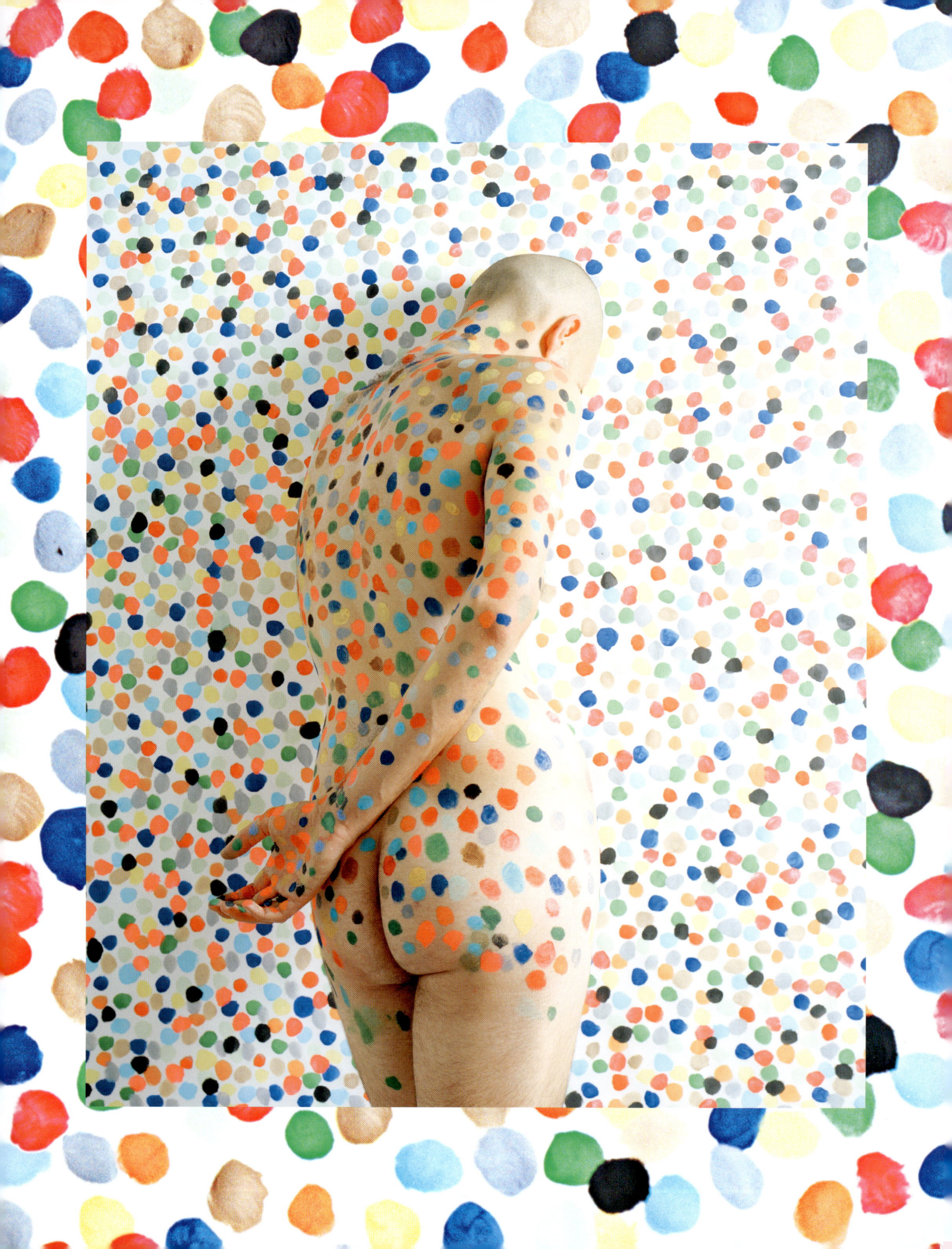

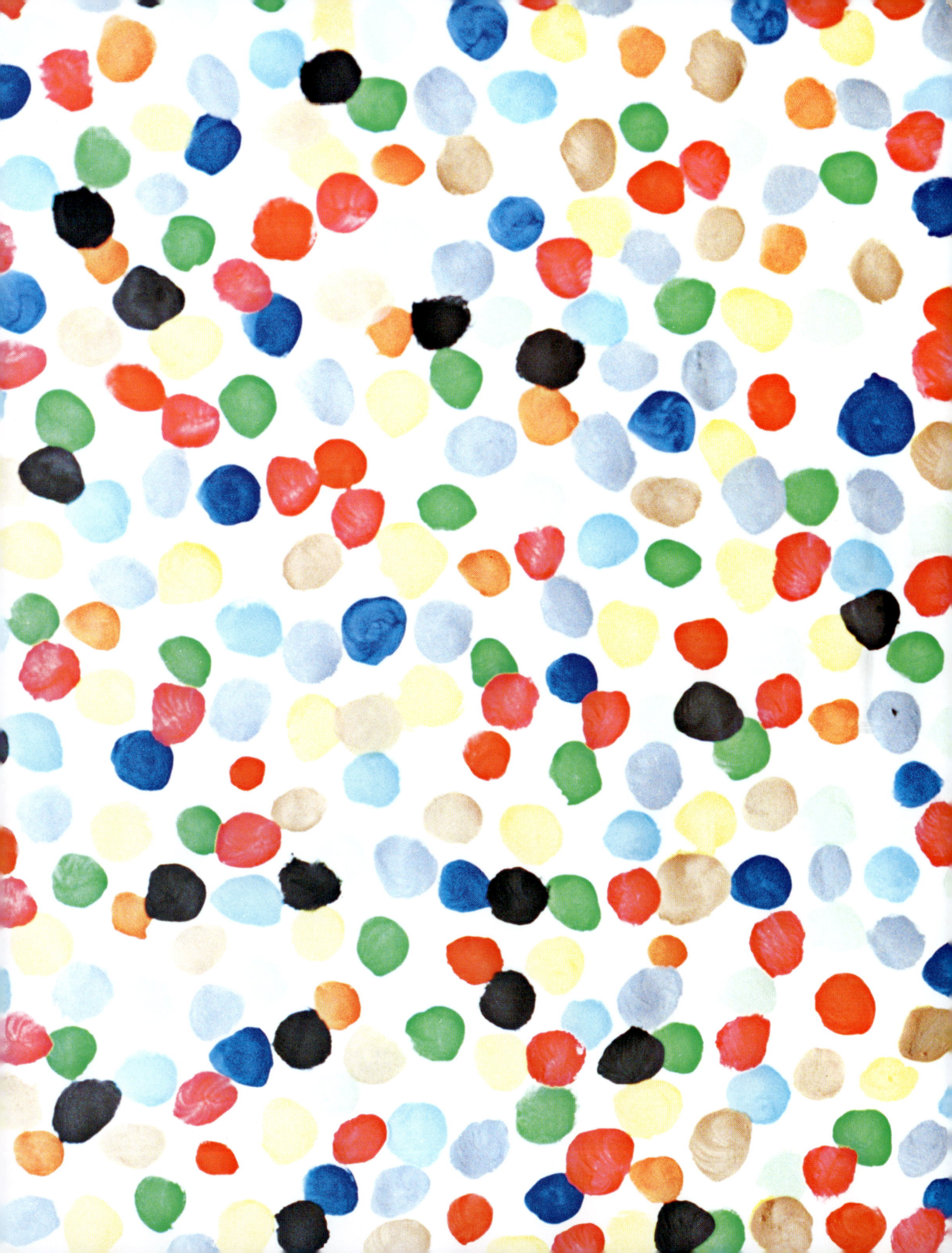

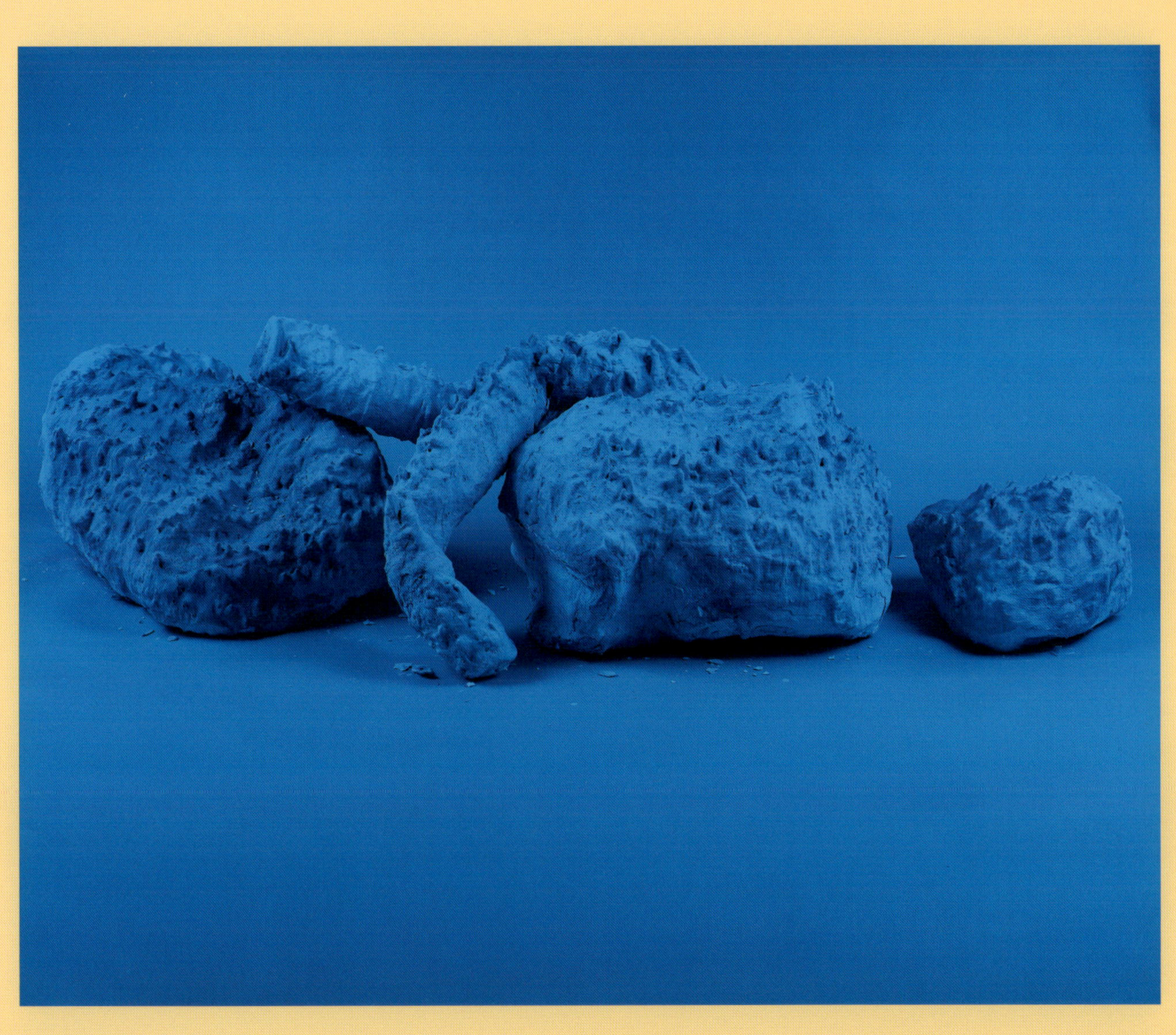

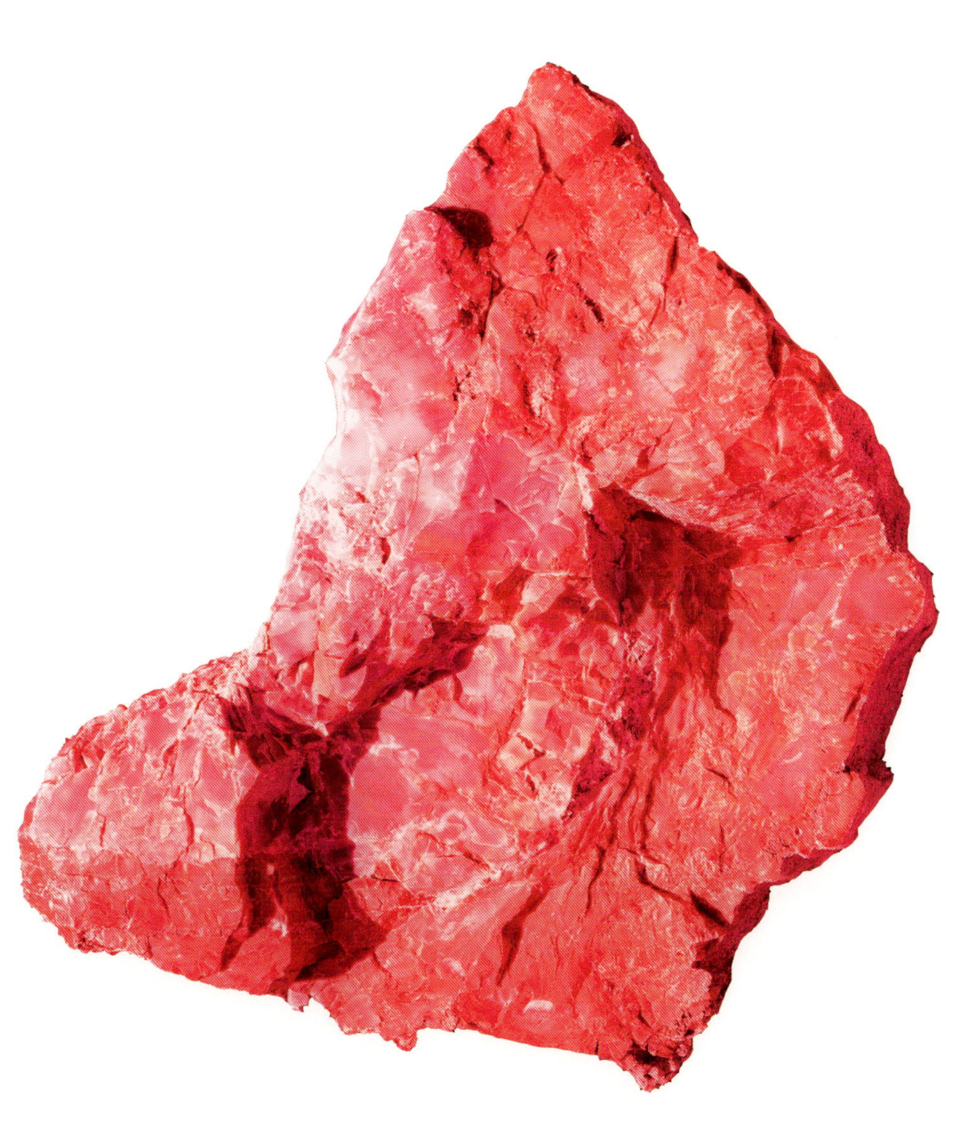

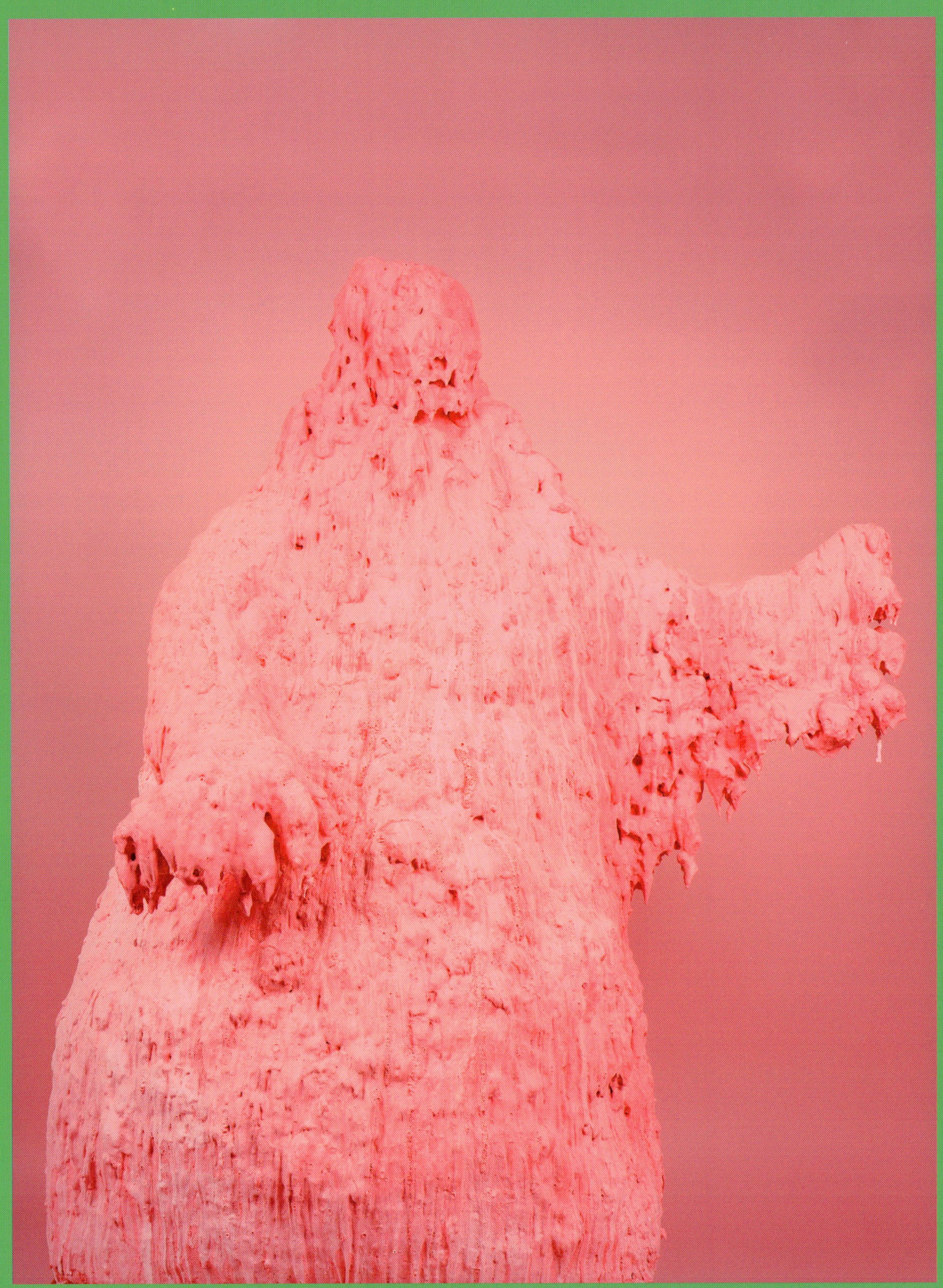

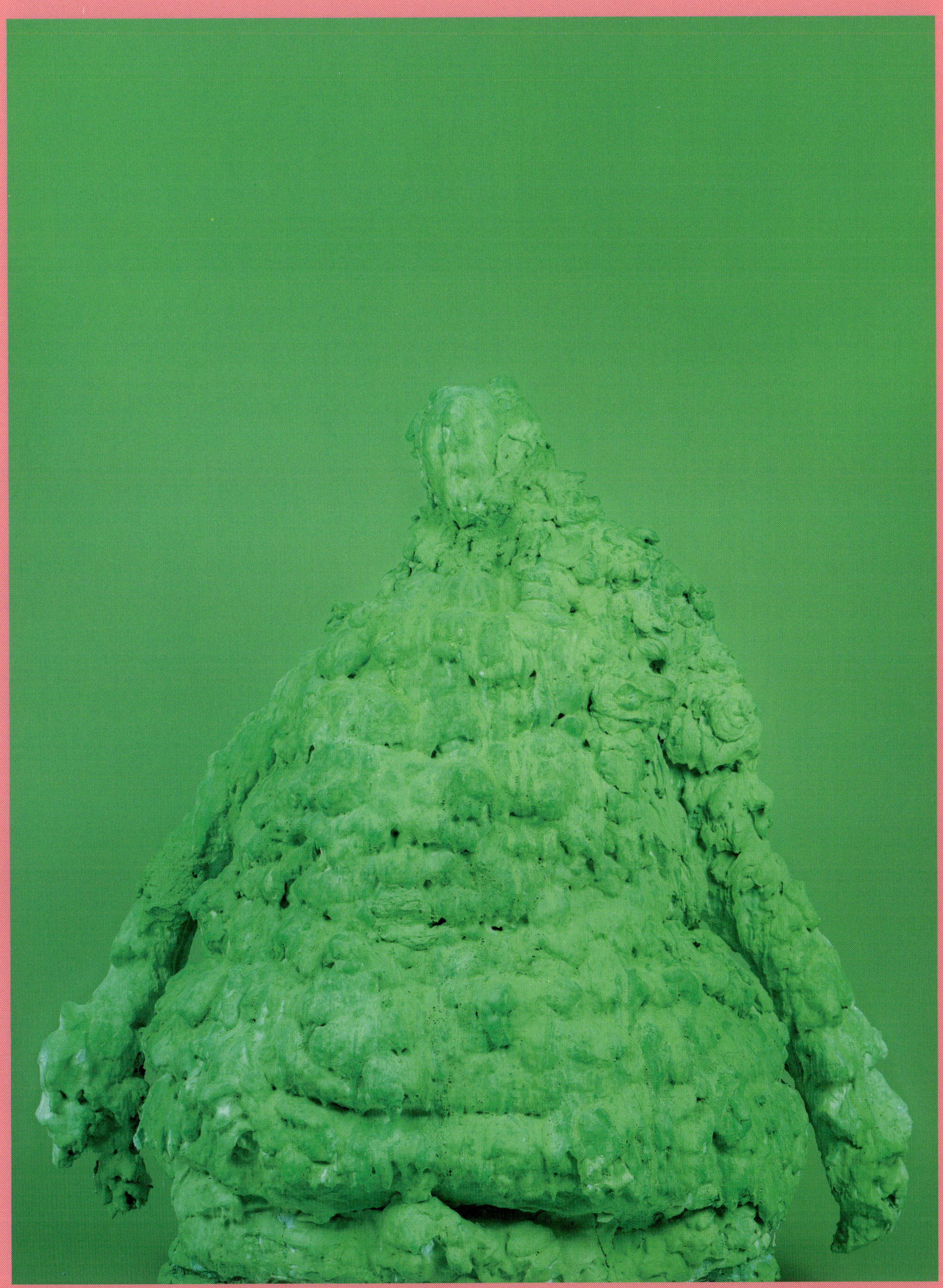

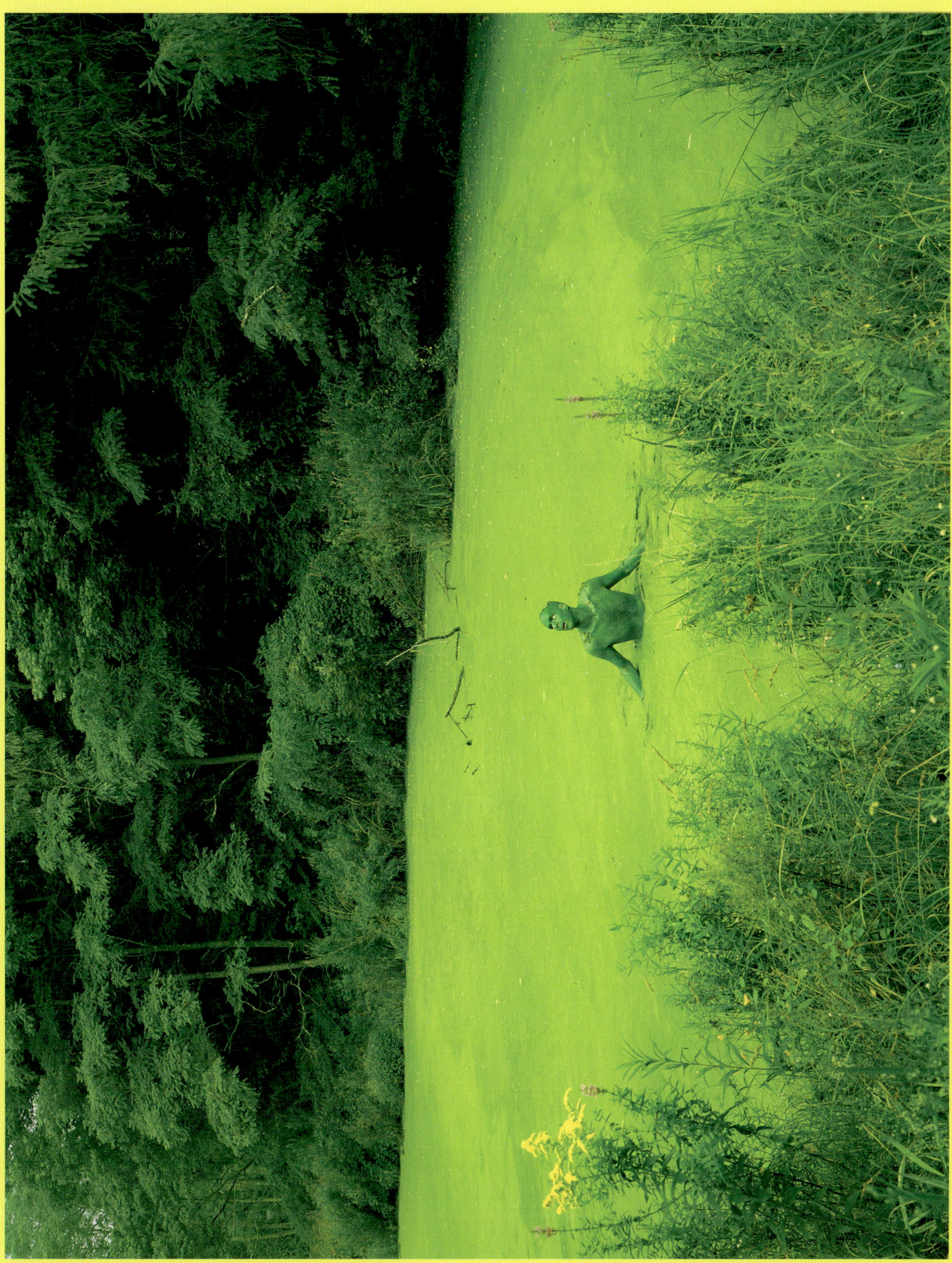

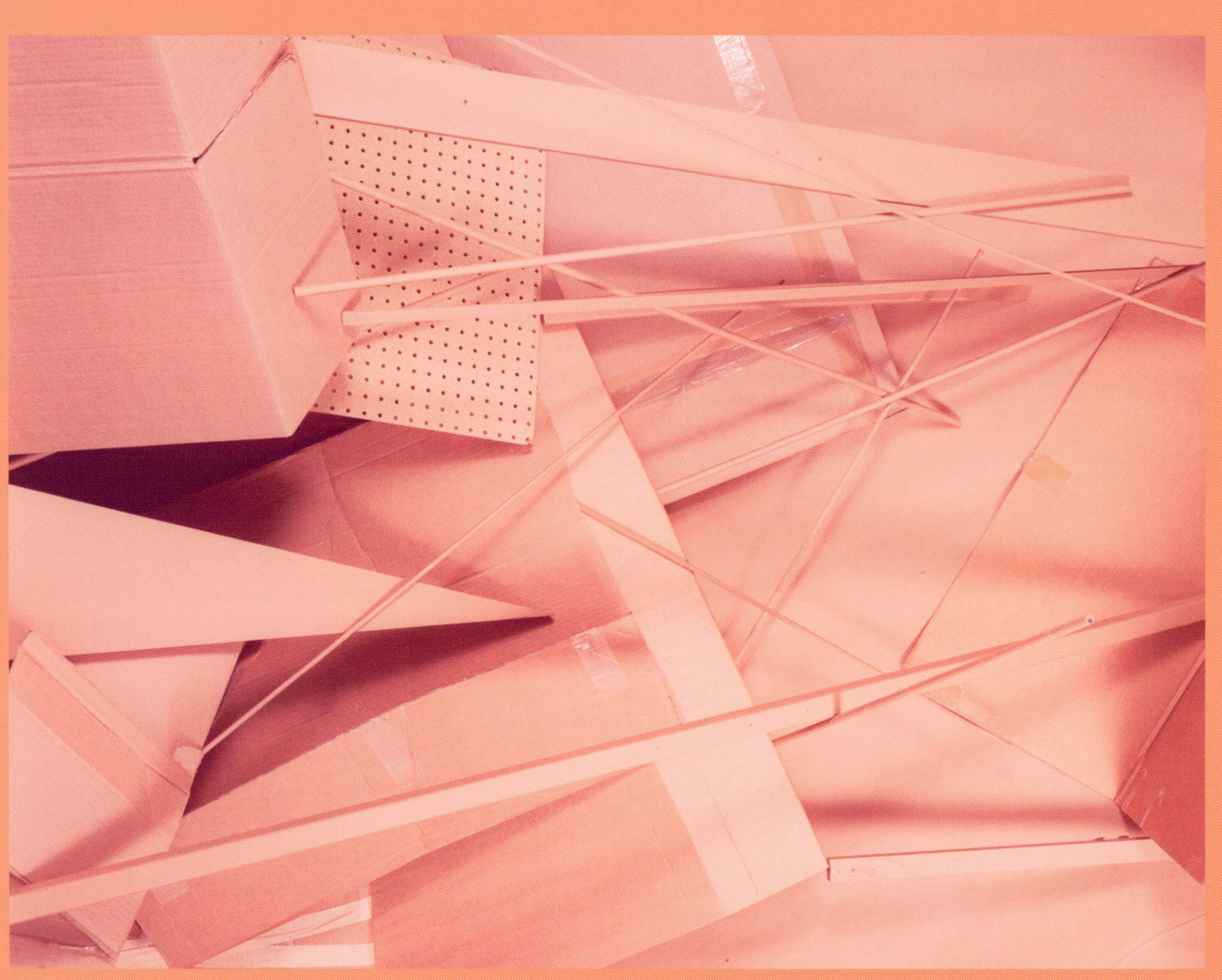

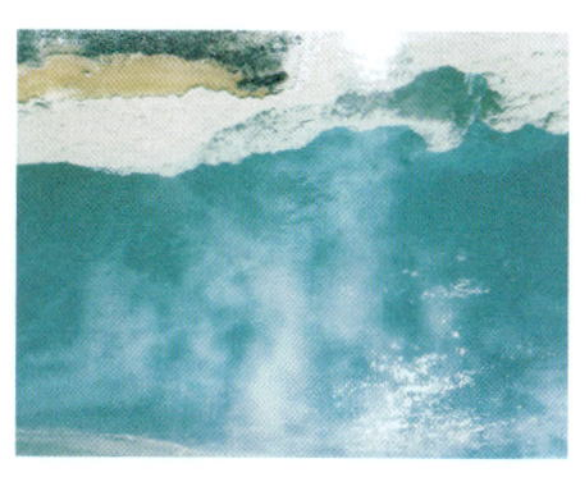 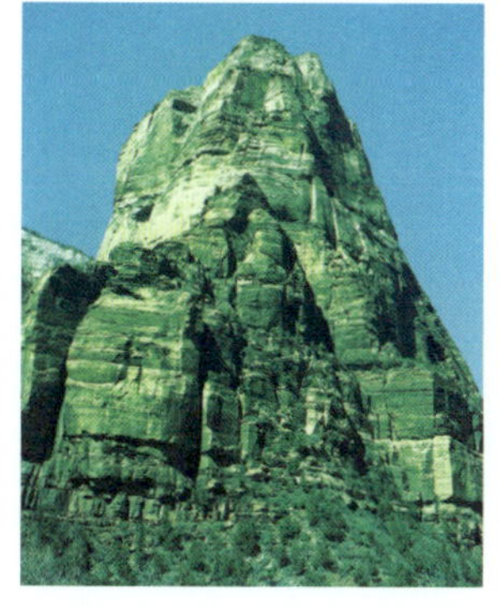

GOAT LAKE SALT LICK , 2011

HOLY HOLY HOLY, 2009

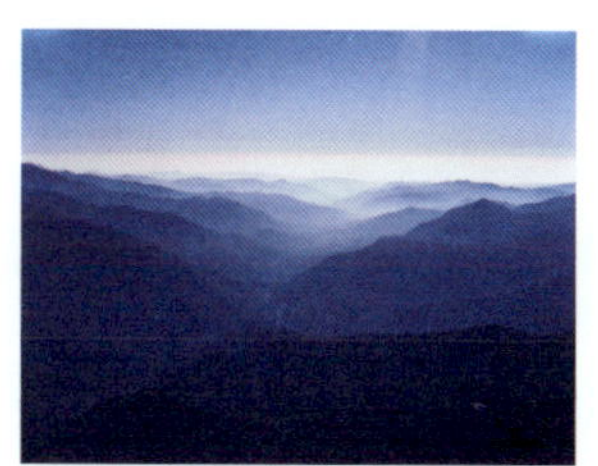

HUNTING HORSEY ALPINE HAZEMEN, 2011

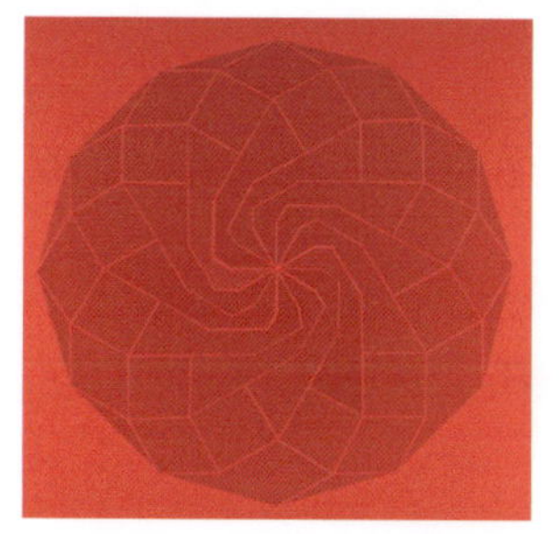 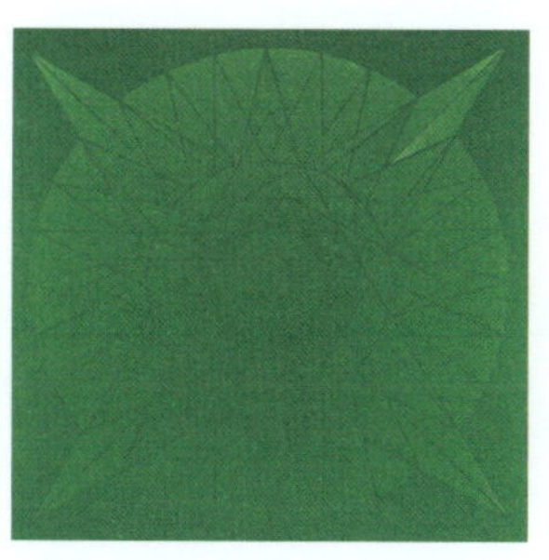

SOLAR SYSTEM IN FIRE SYSTEM, 2011
ANALOG COLOR PHOTOGRAPHIC COLLAGE

SOLAR SYSTEM IN EARTH SYSTEM, 2011
ANALOG COLOR PHOTOGRAPHIC COLLAGE

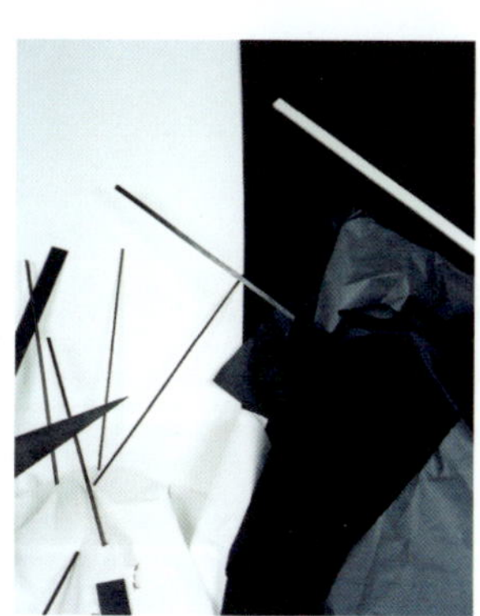

**BLACK AND WHITE LIGHT CONFUSION
(NEWYORK), 2011**

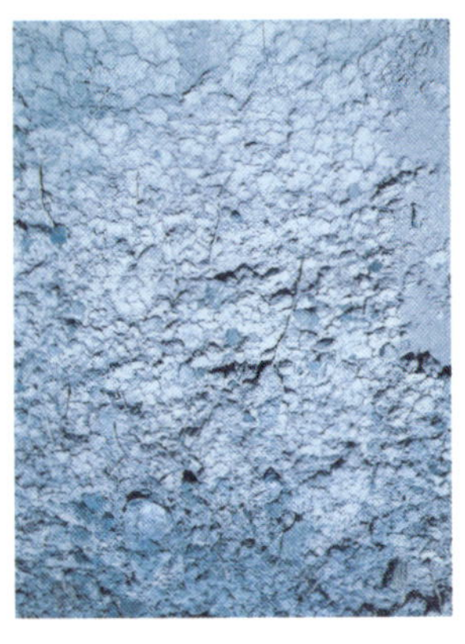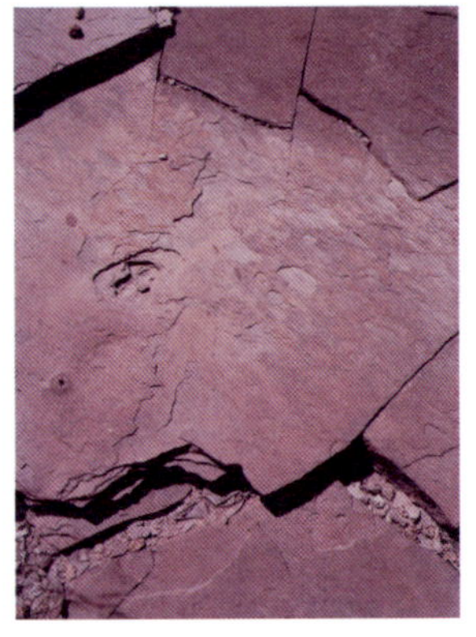

BLUE BORON DULL DEFINITE, 2011

THROWING SHIFTING SHADE SHALE, 2011

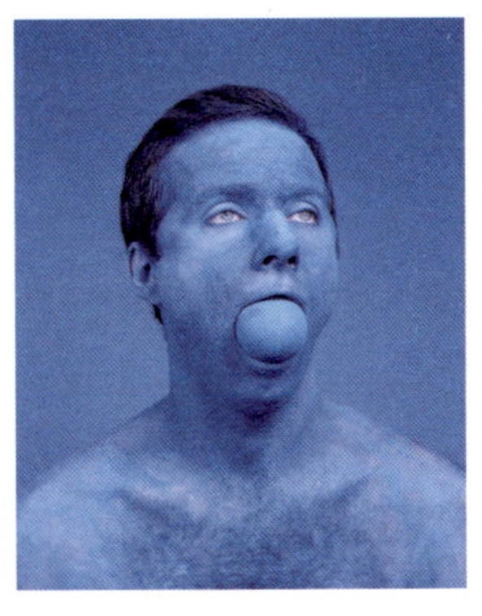

BLUEBALLS, 2010

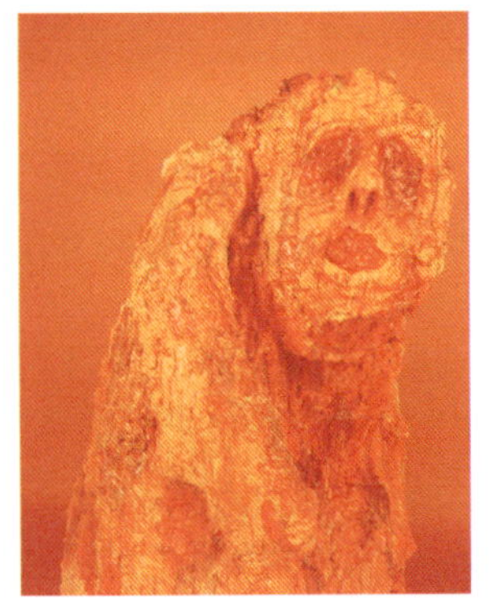

HOW COULD I HAVE EVER LOST YOU, 2010

**BLOOD BURNED RUSTED ROSE STAINED
SCARLET SEDIMENT, 2011**

SOLAR SYSTEM IN AIR SYSTEM, 2011
ANALOG COLOR PHOTOGRAPHIC COLLAGE

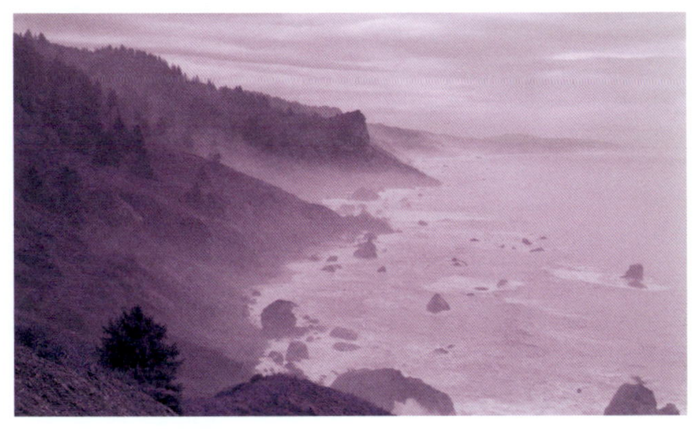

ALL MATTERINGS OF MIND EQUAL ONE
VIOLET, 2011

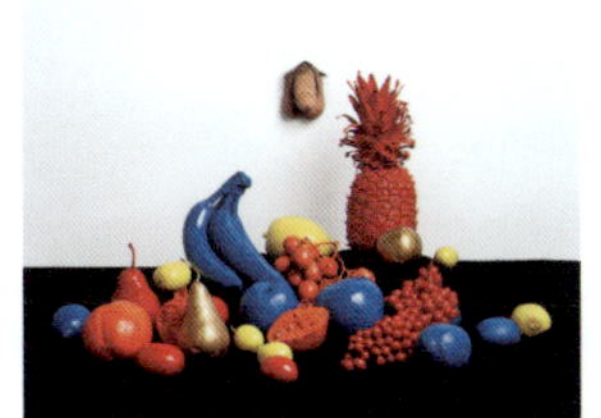

TOUCHED BY THE HAND OF GOD, 2009

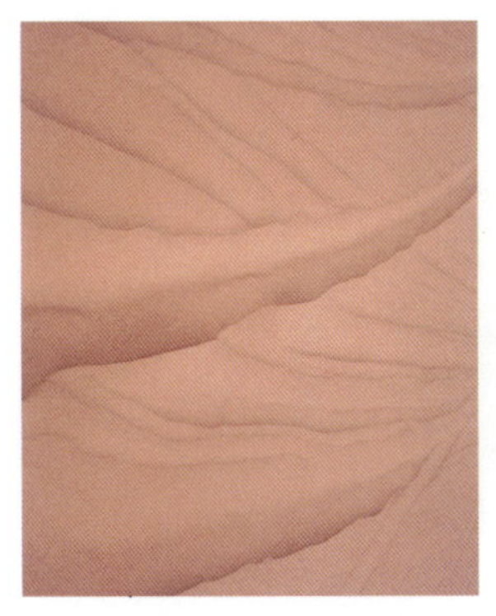

JET TRAIL SAND PALE, 2011

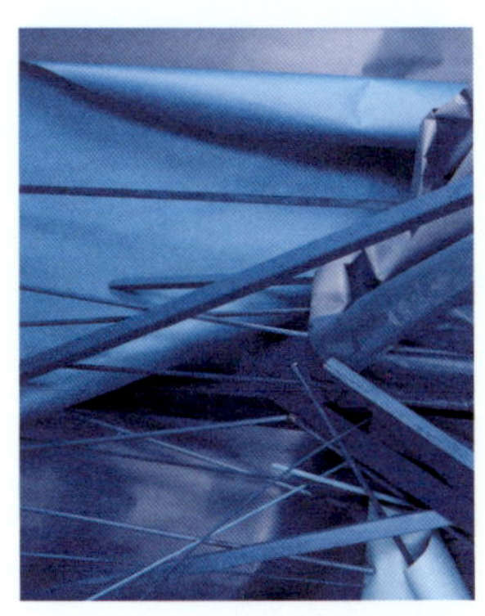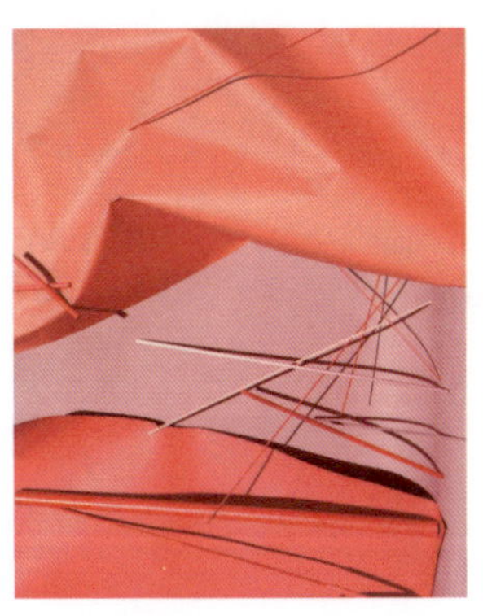

INDIGO LIGHT CONFUSION (NEW YORK), 2011

FORCED FORMICA LIGHT SOFT CONFUSION, 2011

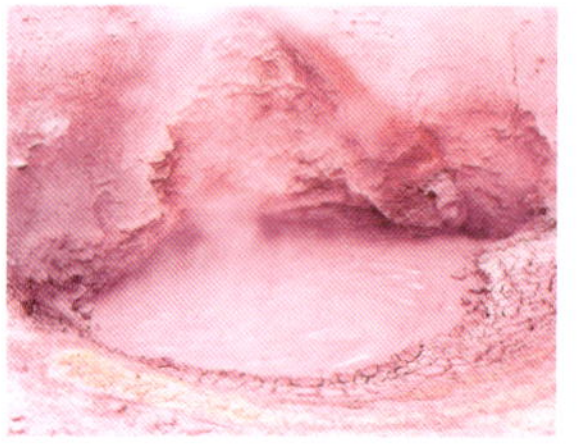

PANDEMONIUM PERFECT WORLD, 2011

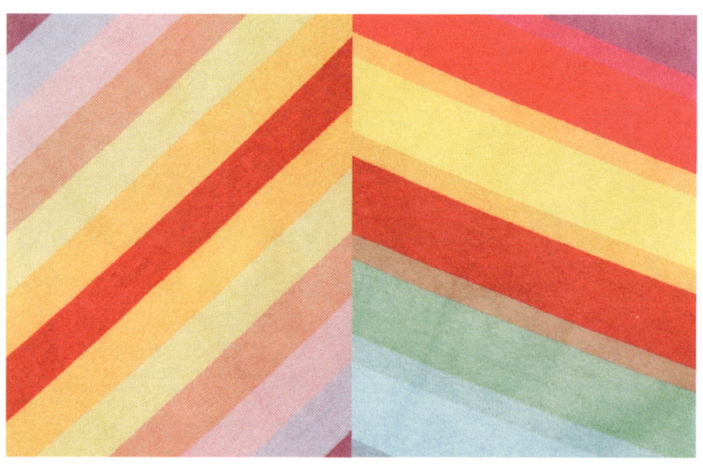

QUANTUM LIGHT, 2011

QUANTUM LIGHT II, 2011

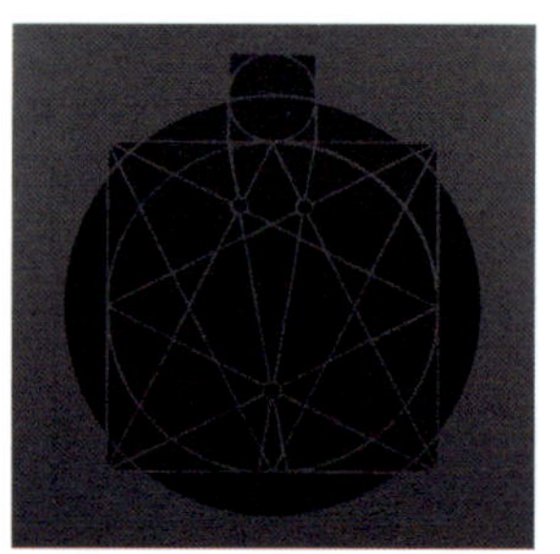

SOLAR SYSTEM IN VOID SYSTEM, 2011
ANALOG COLOR PHOTOGRAPHIC COLLAGE

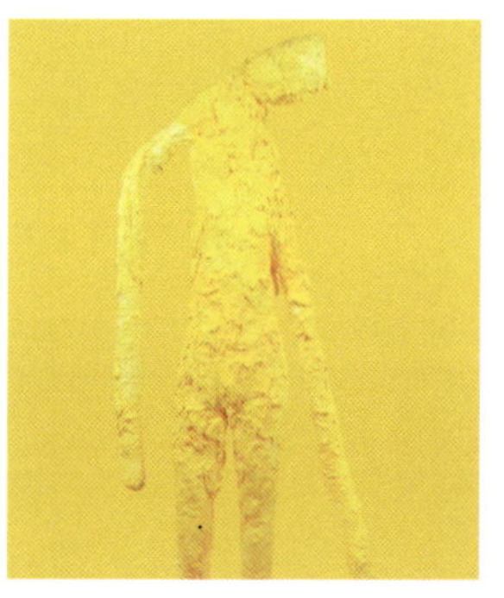

GOLDEN GOD ROD RADIANT LEMON LACTATING
SAFFRON SAP, 2011

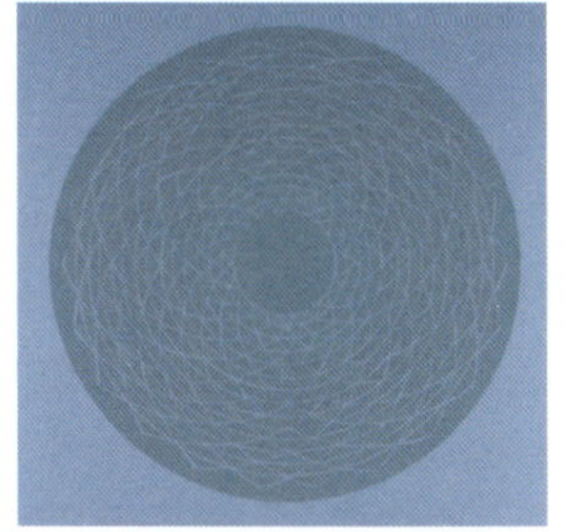

SOLAR SYSTEM IN WATER SYSTEM, 2011
ANALOG COLOR PHOTOGRAPHIC COLLAGE

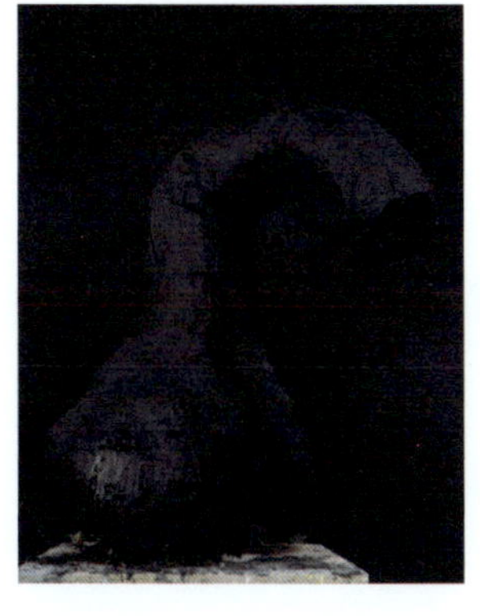

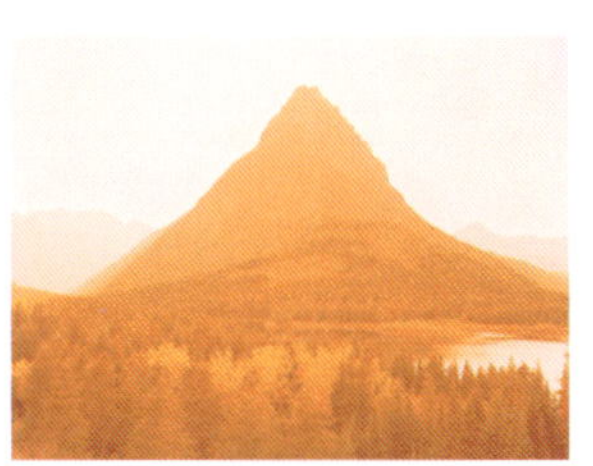

**PREGNANT PULP VOID VACCINATED
OBSIDIAN OH MORTAL MELT, 2011**

ERECTED WRECKED ERECTION MESS, 2011

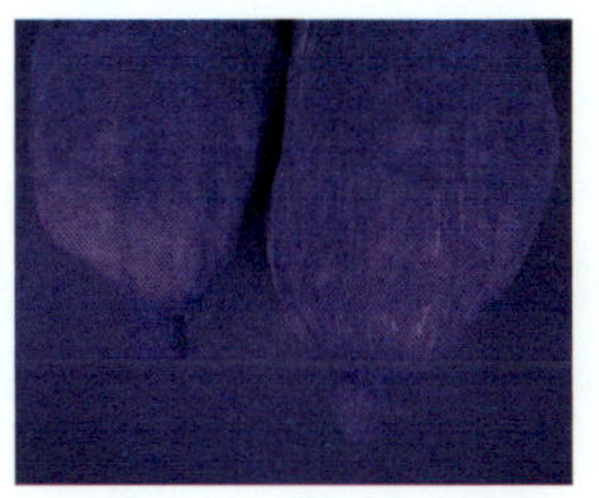

**ACTIVE AMETHYST AFTERNOON IN INDIGO
IDENTITY IDEAL ICE, 2011**

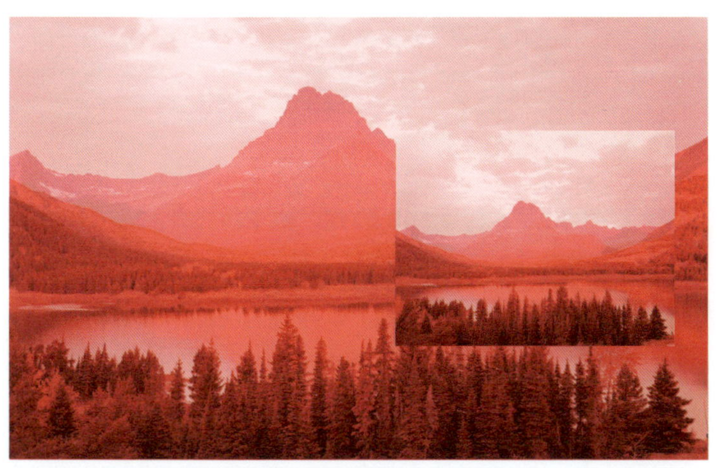

ULTIMATE EARTH EYELESS SKY, 2011

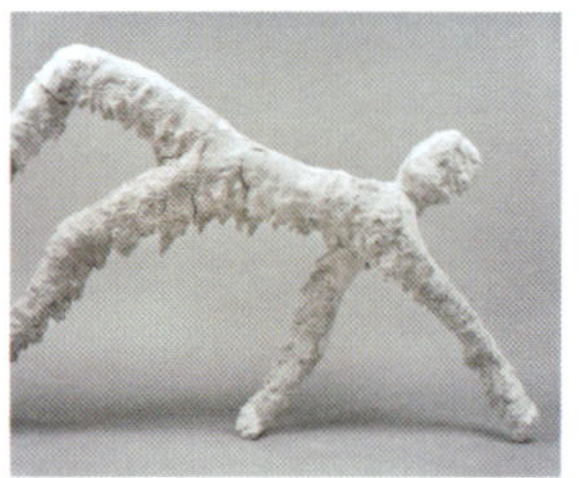

ARCTIC ARSENIC CHARCOAL CHAFFING SLATE
SOAKED WARM WORMED WALKER, 2011

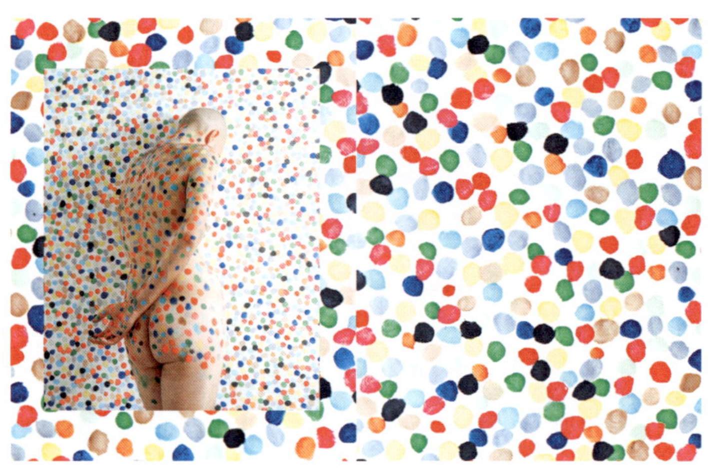

BIRTH IN FUTUREVERSE, 2009

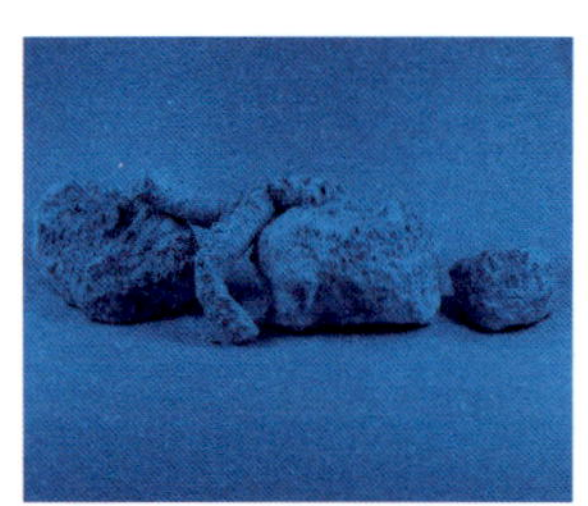

ROYAL RUIN ULTRAMARINE UMBILICAL
FIEND FALLEN COBALT CORE, 2011

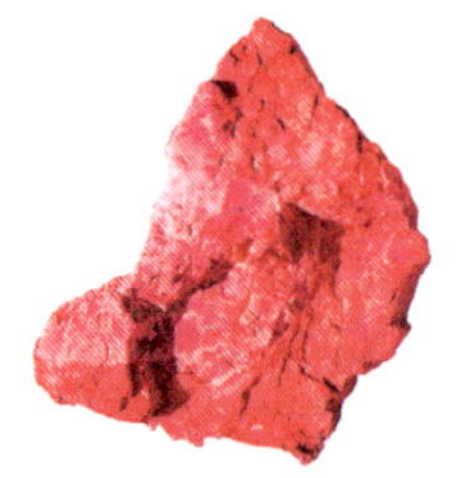

I KNOW YOU LOVE ONE PERSON SO WHY
CAN'T YOU LOVE TWO, 2010

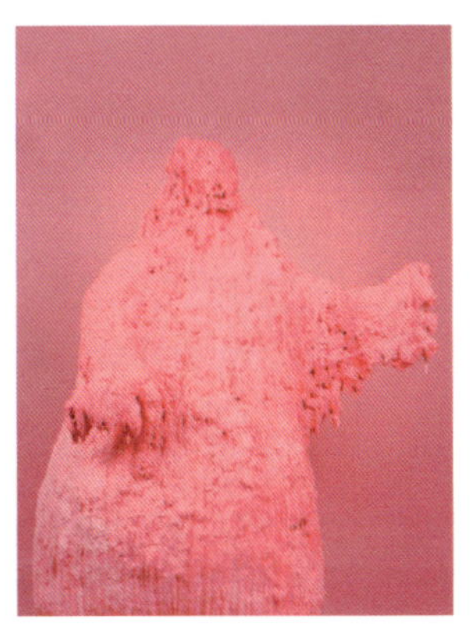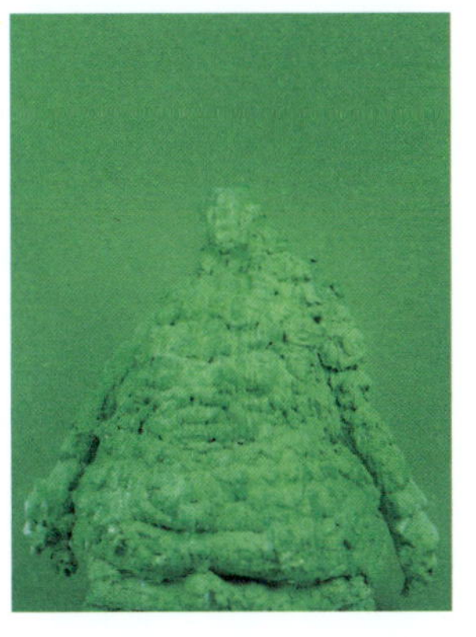

FUCHSIA FUTURE BISMUTH BOILED PUCE
POISED CALIFORNIA CORAL SAND STONE, 2011

JADE JUICED EMERALD EARTHQUAKE FORESKIN
FOREST MOSS MOLD, 2011

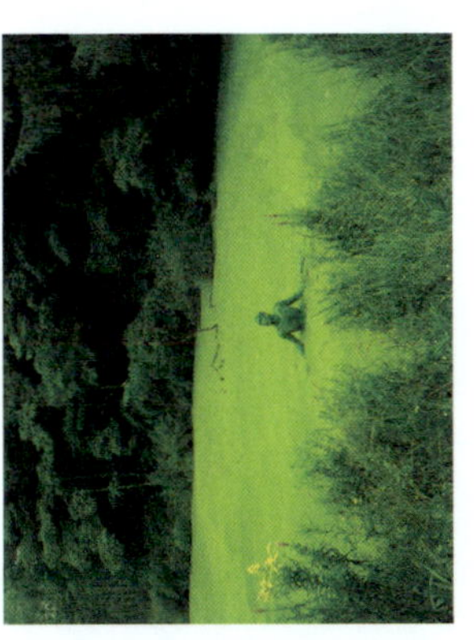

SELF PORTRAIT AS THE BORN FEELING
BEGINS, 2009

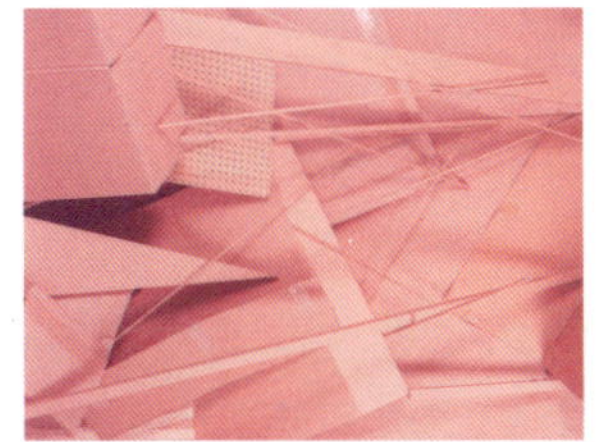

DESERT ROSE LIGHT CONFUSION (UTAH), 2011

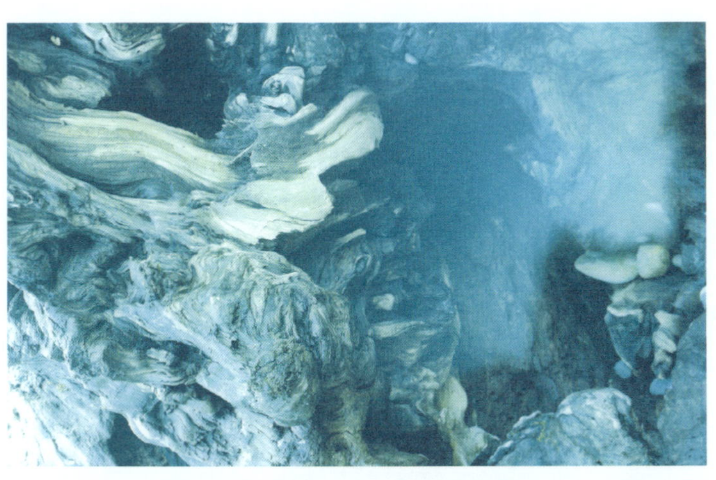

MINTED SENSORIA, 2009

David Benjamin Sherry
Quantum Light

ISBN 978-88-6208-213-6

Published by Damiani and Salon 94

Printed in December 2011 by Grafiche Damiani, Bologna, Italy
Graphic design and concept by Tiffany Malakooti
Conversation edited by Alexis Quinlan and Simon Greenberg
Color correction by My Own Color Lab, New York

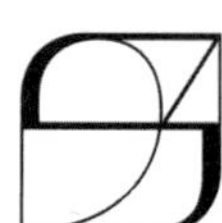

DAMIANI

Damiani editore
via Zanardi, 376
40131 Bologna, Italy
t +39 051 63 56 811
info@damianieditore.it
www.damianieditore.com

Salon 94
243 Bowery
New York, NY 10002
t +1 212 979 0001
info@salon94.com
www.salon94.com

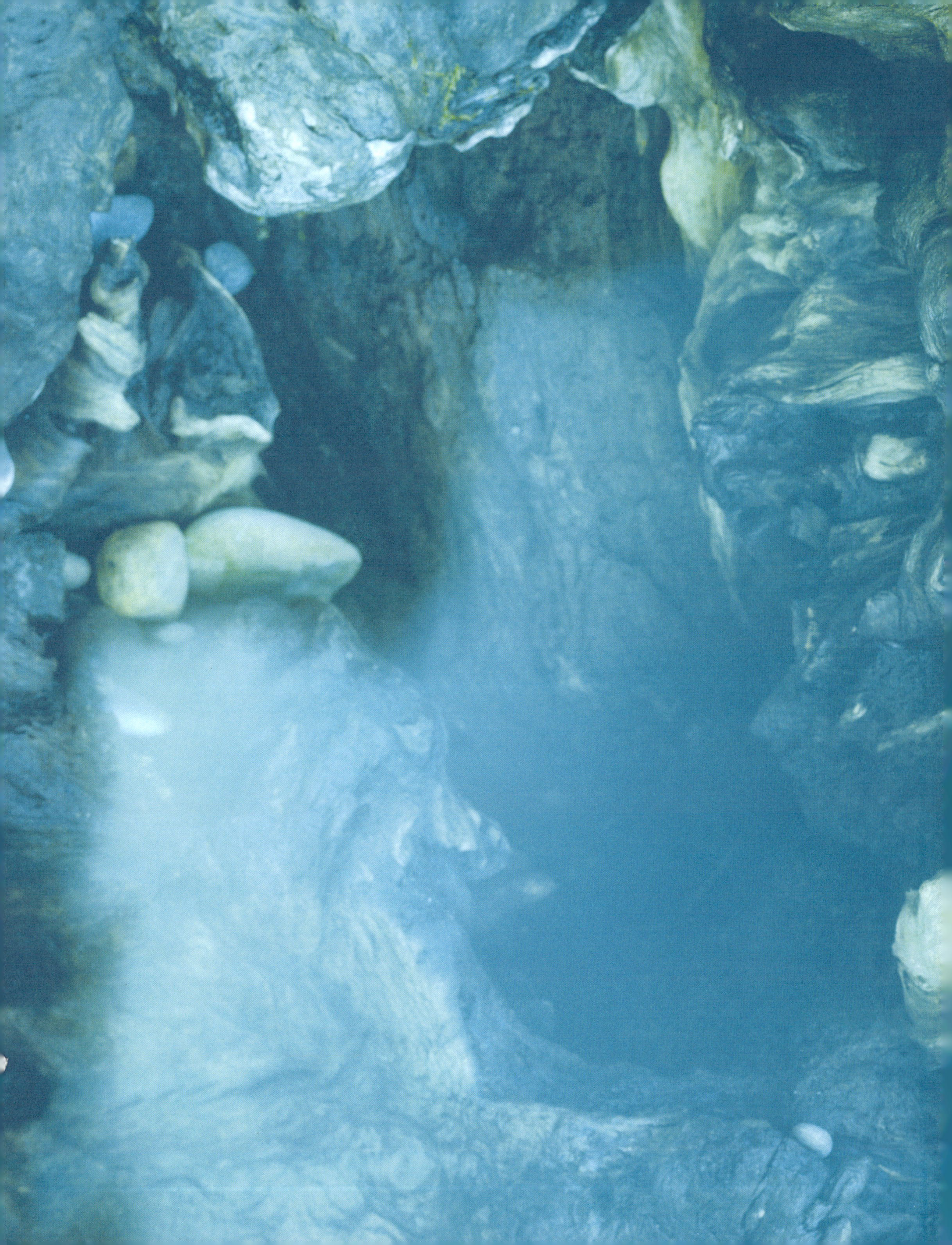